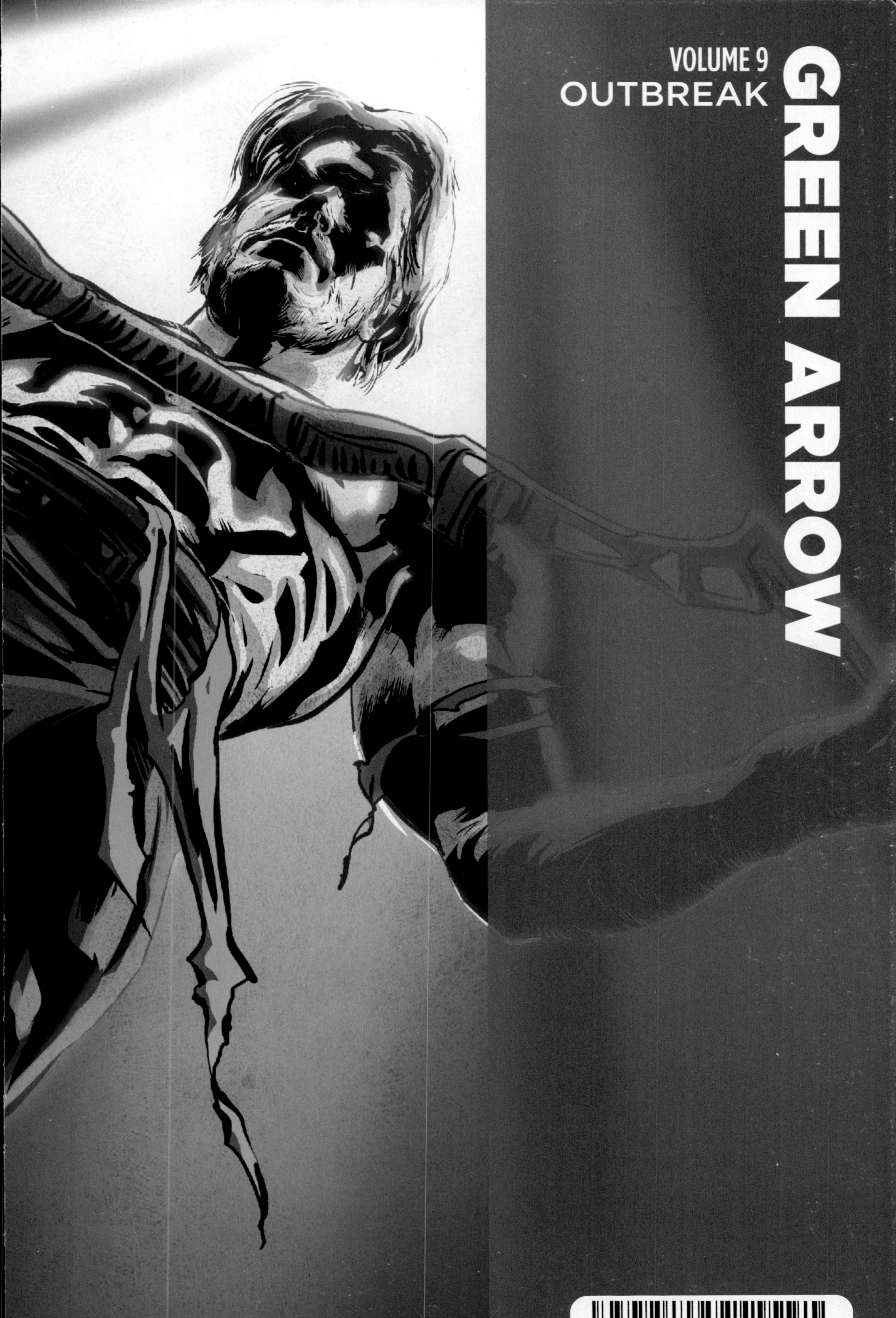

GREEN ARROW

VOLUME 9

OUTBREAK

GREEN ARROW

VOLUME 9
OUTBREAK

WRITTEN BY
BENJAMIN PERCY

ART BY
SZYMON KUDRANSKI
PATRICK ZIRCHER

COLOR BY
GABE ELTAEB

LETTERS BY
ROB LEIGH
DAVE SHARPE

COLLECTION COVER ART BY
SZYMON KUDRANSKI

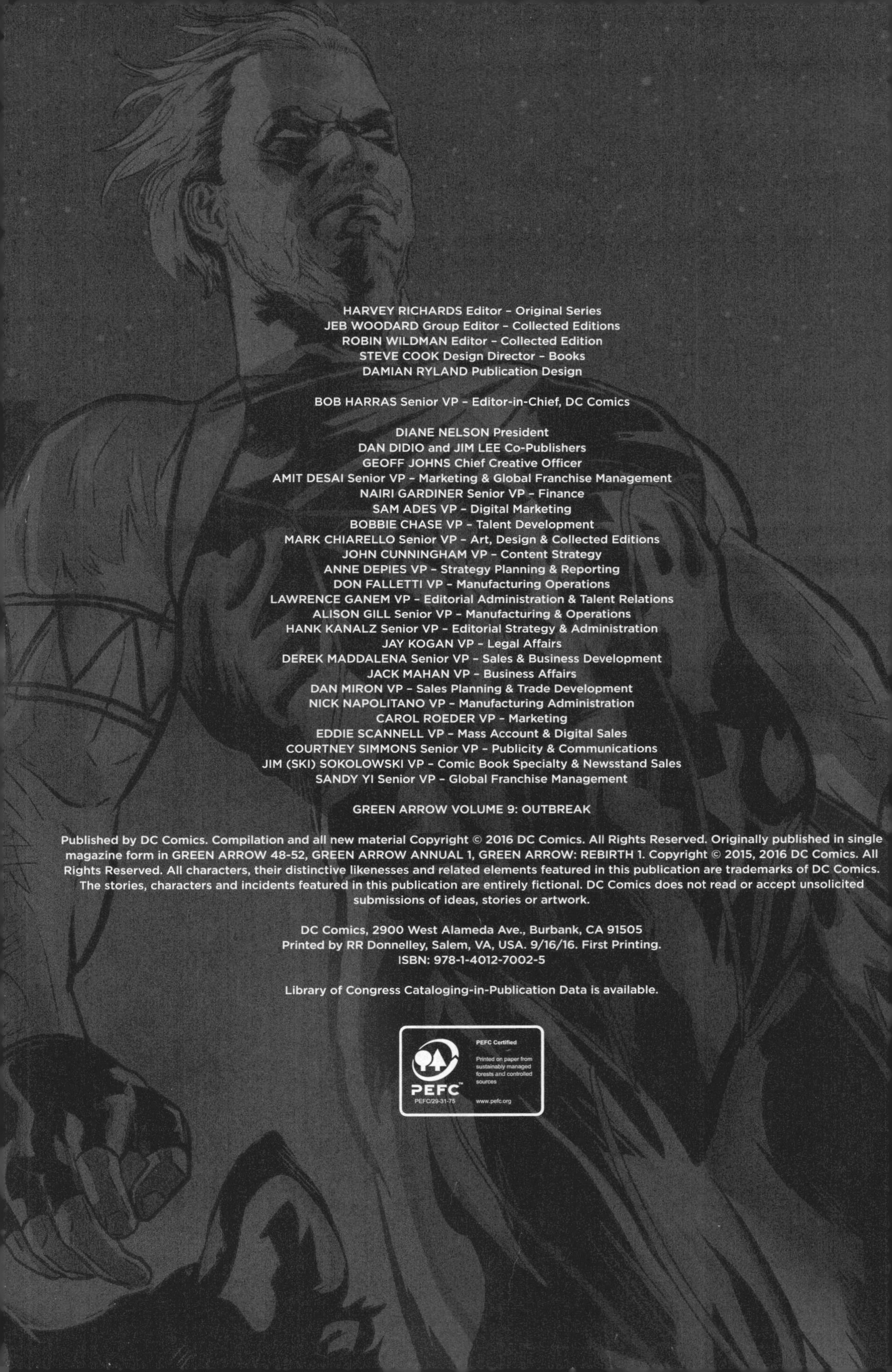

GREEN ARROW VOLUME 9: OUTBREAK

DC Comics, 2900 West Alameda Ave., Burbank, CA 91505
Printed by RR Donnelley, Salem, VA, USA. 9/16/16. First Printing.
ISBN: 978-1-4012-7002-5

Library of Congress Cataloging-in-Publication Data is available.

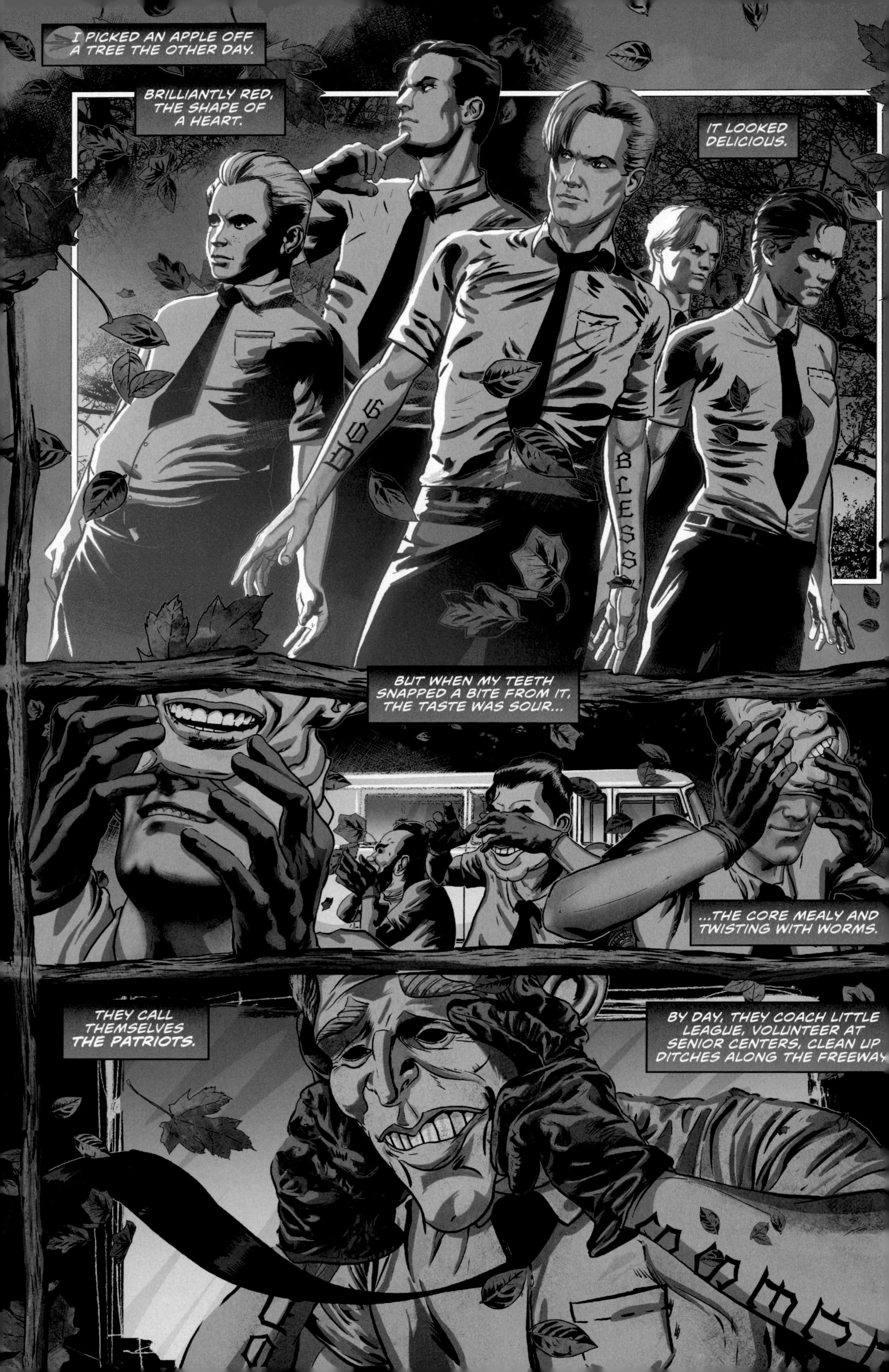
I PICKED AN APPLE OFF A TREE THE OTHER DAY.
BRILLIANTLY RED, THE SHAPE OF A HEART.
IT LOOKED DELICIOUS.
BLESS
BUT WHEN MY TEETH SNAPPED A BITE FROM IT, THE TASTE WAS SOUR...
...THE CORE MEALY AND TWISTING WITH WORMS.
THEY CALL THEMSELVES THE PATRIOTS.
BY DAY, THEY COACH LITTLE LEAGUE, VOLUNTEER AT SENIOR CENTERS, CLEAN UP DITCHES ALONG THE FREEWAY

Seattle
AND BY NIGHT?
THEY REVEAL THEIR TRUE SELVES, THEIR HEARTS ROTTEN WITH WRITHING, BLACK WORMS.
REGISTER of the INFECTED
Seattle, WA
Johnny Evision
13 Jurgens Village
Seattle, WA 98105
THIS IS NO DIFFERENT THAN WEEDING LAWNS, SCRAPING GUM OFF DESKS, COLLECTING BEER CANS FROM ALLEYS.
WE'RE CLEANING UP THE FILTH.
SPREAD OUT. HIT AS MANY ADDRESSES AS YOU CAN. THIS PLACE IS A HIVE.
REGROUP AT THE VAN IN FIVE MINUTES!

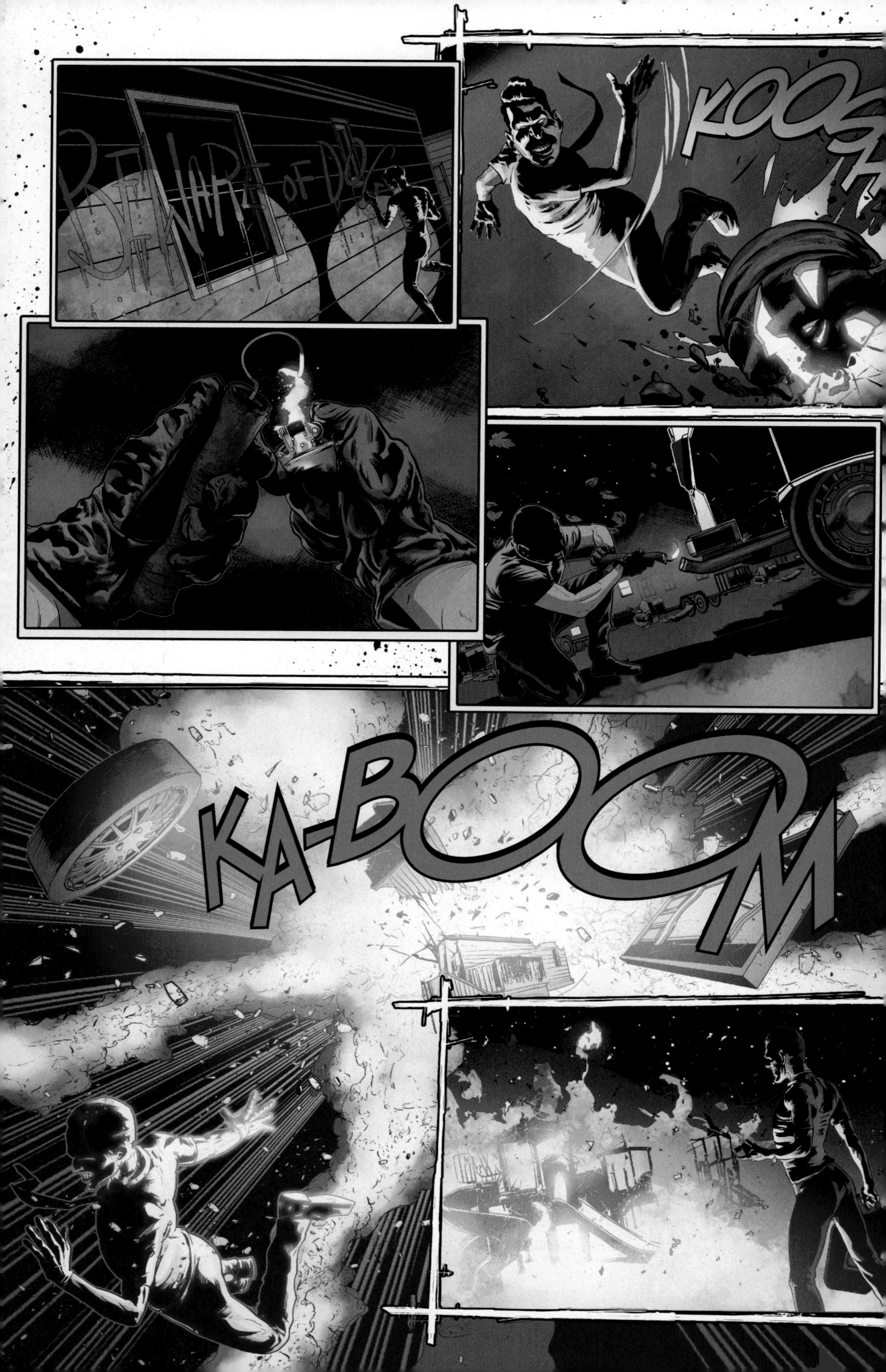
BEWARE OF DOG
KA-BOOM

IT'S DR. JEKYLL AND MR. HYDE, YOU IDIOTS!
CRASH
NO!
THE CATEGORY IS MONSTERS IN LITERATURE.
HEEL, MUTT! HEEL!

THAT THING YOU DID? BEFORE THE OTHER THING. I DON'T KNOW WHAT THAT WAS, BUT DAMN...
OLIVER QUEEN'S APARTMENT...
...WHER ARE YO GOING?
HOME.
STAY THE NIGHT, MELANIE. I'LL MAKE YOU WAFFLES. I'LL KISS YOU WITH MY NASTY MORNING BREATH.
THAT SOUNDS LIKE SOMETHING TWO PEOPLE WOULD DO IF THEY'RE SERIOUS ABOUT EACH OTHER, PRETENDING TO BE MARRIED, SEEING HOW IT GOES.
BUT... WAFFLES...
THAT WAS FUN, OLLIE, BUT LET'S FACE IT: YOU'RE RICH, YOU'RE HOT, YOU'RE WHITE, YOU'RE MALE. YOU'VE GOT A HUGE--
APARTMENT?
YOU'RE NOT REAL.
YOU'RE NOT SOMEONE ANYONE CAN RELATE TO.

SIX MONTHS AGO, ON THE OUTSKIRTS OF THE RAINIER WILDERNESS, A WOLF ATTACKED SEVERAL HIKERS, A RANCHER AND A RANGER.
IT WAS NOT RABID.
THERE WAS SOMETHING ELSE WRONG WITH IT. AN OLD, FORGOTTEN DISEASE--CALLED LUKOS.
IT SPREAD TO DOZENS OF PEOPLE IN WASHINGTON BEFORE IT WAS CONTAINED.
THE INFECTED--CLASSIFIED AS THE WARGS--WERE MEDICATED AND PUT BY THE STATE INTO A SECRET, ISOLATING PROTECTION PROGRAM.
BEWARE OF DOG
WHEN THE MEDIA STARTED ASKING QUESTIONS, THE GOVERNMENT SAID THEY WERE BASICALLY OFFERING EXPERIMENTAL CLINICS FOR SOME RABIES PATIENTS.
WE DON'T KNOW HOW THEY FOUND YOU, MISTER EVISION.
GO HOME DOG!!
I HEARD THERE WAS A DATA BREACH AT THE HOSPITAL. NOW THE HACKERS HAVE LEAKED OUR NAMES AND ADDRESSES ONLINE.
I DON'T KNOW ANYTHING ABOUT THAT.
I CAN'T WORK. I CAN'T TRAVEL. SUPPOSEDLY FOR OTHER PEOPLE'S SAFETY. BUT WHAT ABOUT MINE?
JUST CONTINUE TO TAKE YOUR MEDICATION AND KNOW WE'RE IN THE PROCESS OF FINDING A NEW LOCATION FOR YOU AND YOUR PEOPLE.
MIND ME ASKING HOW'D YOU GET INFECTED?
I SLEPT WITH THE WRONG... PERSON.
GUESS YOU WERE ASKING FOR IT THEN.
I FEEL LIKE I NEED TO WEAR A HAZMAT SUIT AROUND THESE FREAKS.
I HEAR YOU.

GREEN ARROW'S HQ...
I'M HEARING SOME RUMBLINGS ABOUT AN ATTACK ON A LUKOS SAFE HAVEN. DUDES IN PRESIDENT MASKS. WHITE VAN, NO PLATES.
ANOTHER HATE CRIME. SOMEBODY'S GOING TO GET KILLED IF THIS KEEPS UP.
THE STATE DOESN'T HAVE THE BUDGET OR THE MANPOWER TO PROTECT THE WARGS. GREEN ARROW MAY WANT TO LOOK INTO THIS.
I HEAR THE WORDS COMING OUT OF YOUR MOUTH, FYFF, BUT THEY'RE DIFFICULT TO PROCESS WHILE YOU'RE SITTING ON THAT RIDICULOUS BALL.
THE DOCTOR SAID IT WILL TIGHTEN UP MY CORE, HELP WITH MY BACK PAIN.
YOU WANT TO TRY IT OUT? IT'S KIND OF FUN. BOUNCY.
I WOULD NEVER SIT ON ANYTHING YOU'VE SAT ON.
WHAT CAN YOU TELL ME ABOUT LUKOS? THIS IS SOME SORT OF NEW DISEASE?
WHAT AM I, *WIKIPEDIA?*
PRETTY MUCH. I POKE YOU, INFORMATION SPILLS OUT.
"YOU'RE NOT THE ONLY ONE IN THE DARK. I'VE BEEN READING UP ON SOME FILES. NO ONE KNOWS WHEN LUKOS BEGAN, BUT THEY GUESS THE SEVENTH CENTURY..."
"...AND THEY DON'T KNOW EXACTLY WHERE, BUT THEY GUESS SCANDINAVIA."

"WHAT THEY DO KNOW FOR CERTAIN IS THAT IT CAME FROM A WOLF INFECTED WITH A WASTING DISEASE.
"ON THE SOLSTICE, IN CERTAIN NORTHERN TERRITORIES, PEOPLE WOULD CHOW DOWN THE BRAIN AND HEART OF THE ANIMAL...
"...BELIEVING ITS POWER WOULD HELP THEM SURVIVE THE LONG WINTER AHEAD.
"IN THIS WAY, HE INFECTION SPREAD AND UTATED IN ITS HUMAN HOST.
"IT DEFORMED THE FRONTAL LOBE AND SWELLED THE ADRENAL AND PITUITARY GLANDS.
"A DISEASE THAT BELONGED TO ANGER, HUNGER, IMPULSIVITY.
"THEY HAD WOLVES IN THEIR BELLIES, I GUESS YOU COULD SAY."

"THE INFECTED NORSE BECAME SOME OF THE MOST FEARED WARRIORS IN HISTORY.
"KNOWN SOMETIMES AS BERSERKERS, OTHER TIMES AS WARGS, THE TERM COMMONLY USED TODAY.
"THEY FOUGHT WITH UNCONTROLLABLE FURY.
"WHEN EXCITED, ENRAGED, THEIR EYES AND NOSE AND GUMS AND FINGERNAILS BLED.
"THAT'S HOW THE DISEASE PROPAGATED ITSELF--BY THE HUNDREDS, THE THOUSANDS, THE MILLIONS.
"THE LONGER THE INFECTION, THE GREATER THE CHANGE.
"AND THEN THE WORLD BEGAN TO BITE BACK.
"THE WARGS WERE SLAUGHTERED DURING THE CRUSADES.
"TRIED BY THE PURITANS.
TARNOW
USCHWITZ
SS
"AND FINALLY EXTINGUISHED BY HITLER'S ARMY."

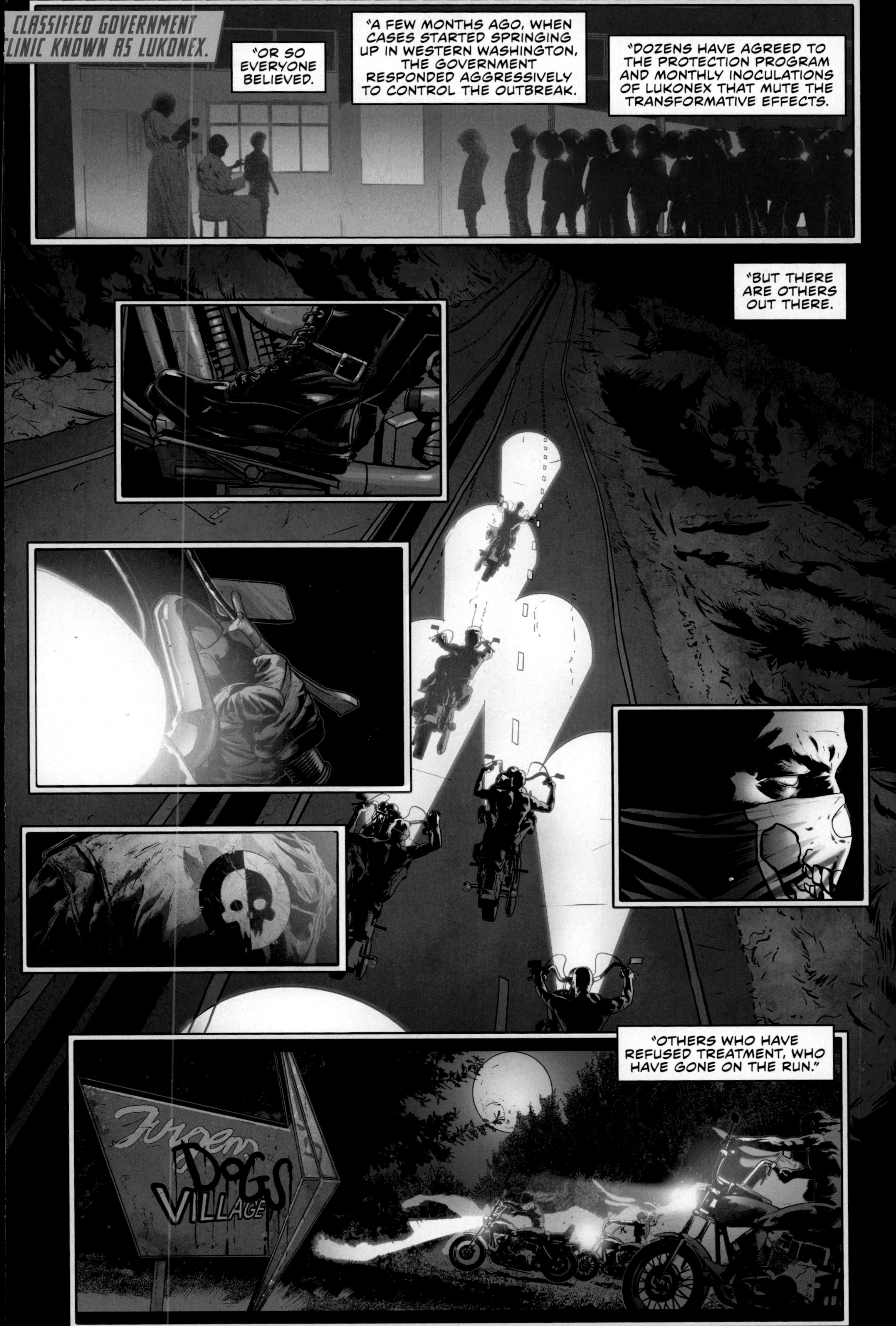
CLASSIFIED GOVERNMENT
LINIC KNOWN AS LUKONEX.
"OR SO EVERYONE BELIEVED.
"A FEW MONTHS AGO, WHEN CASES STARTED SPRINGING UP IN WESTERN WASHINGTON, THE GOVERNMENT RESPONDED AGGRESSIVELY TO CONTROL THE OUTBREAK.
"DOZENS HAVE AGREED TO THE PROTECTION PROGRAM AND MONTHLY INOCULATIONS OF LUKONEX THAT MUTE THE TRANSFORMATIVE EFFECTS.
"BUT THERE ARE OTHERS OUT THERE.
"OTHERS WHO HAVE REFUSED TREATMENT, WHO HAVE GONE ON THE RUN."
DOGS
VILLAGE

"THEY'VE GONE FROM THE FEARED AND CELEBRATED WARRIORS AT THE CENTER OF AN ARMY...
"...TO THE GLAZE-EYED FREAKS AT THE MARGINS OF EVERY CITY."
YOU JUST GOING TO LET THE WORLD YANK YOUR COLLAR, SHOVE YOUR FACE IN YOUR OWN FILTH, MAKE YOU BELIEVE YOU'RE DISGUSTING?
WHO ARE YOU?
I'M THE *BIG BAD WOLF.*
A.K.A. *DOLPH MARROCK,* UNMEDICATED WARG, FREQUENT FELON AND PRESIDENT OF THE BERSERKERS BIKE CLUB.

TO TALK TO YOU ABOUT TAKING BACK YOUR CITY...
...BY EMBRACING THE TOOTH AND CLAW.
UM, WHAT ARE YOU DOING, EMIKO?
SOMETIMES I HAVE THESE THOUGHTS. LIKE, WHAT IF SOY MILK IS JUST MILK INTRODUCING ITSELF IN SPANISH?
AND WILL I AGE MORE QUICKLY--LIKE PEARS OR PEACHES--IF I WEAR A PAPER BAG OVER MY HEAD?
THEN I WOULDN'T HAVE TO GO TO THAT STUPID, STUPID, STUPID SCHOOL ANYMORE.

YOU WANT TO TALK ABOUT IT?
WELL...
TWO HOURS AGO...
WE SAW YOUR SISTER'S NAME LISTED ONLINE. THEY'RE SAYING SHE'S ONE OF THE INFECTED. DOES IT RUN IN THE FAMILY?
CAN'T BELIEVE THEY EVEN LET YOU COME BACK TO SCHOOL.
YEAH, HOW DO WE KNOW THAT THE MEDICATION EVEN WORKS? YOU COULD BE *PATIENT ZERO* FOR ALL WE KNOW.
BLACK CANARY
Ugh, MY PHYSICS TEXTBOOK WEIGHS A THOUSAND POUNDS.
CAN I *BORROW* THAT FOR A SEC?

DO YOU EAT KIBBLE FOR BREAKFAST, SARA NASH?
RIFFLE
THWAK
Groan
I WOULDN'T HIT A GIRL, BUT YOU MAKE ME WANNA.

PLEASE DO.
IT WOULD ONLY BE FAIR.
THANKS.

LET'S JUST SAY YOU MIGHT BE GETTING A CALL FROM THE PRINCIPAL, GUIDANCE COUNSELOR, SOME CONCERNED PARENTS, AND MAYBE A LAWYER.
DO YOU KNOW IF THEY BY CHANCE DRIVE A WHITE VAN?
THEY'RE SOPHOMORES. NO LICENSES, NOT YET.
I NEED YOU TO WRITE DOWN THEIR NAMES FOR ME.
WHAT, ARE YOU GOING TO GO BEAT THEM UP? I ALREADY GOT *THAT* COVERED.
SOMEBODY'S GOT THE INFECTED IN THEIR CROSSHAIRS. MAYBE THESE GUYS KNOW SOMETHING.
AREN'T YOU GOING TO YELL AT ME NOW?
I GUESS WE'RE BOTH STUCK IN ROLES WE DON'T LIKE.
GEEZ, EMI. I WANT TO BE YOUR BROTHER, BUT YOU KEEP MAKING ME ACT LIKE A FATHER.
EVERY HALLOWEEN, HERE IN SEATTLE, TENS OF THOUSANDS CROWD THE STREETS...
...FOR THE MIDNIGHT PARADE.
EVERYONE'S GETTING READY FOR IT NOW.
AND THE NOISE IN THE STREET--COPS SETTING UP BARRICADES, VENDORS ARRANGING BOOTHS, PEOPLE STAKING OUT THEIR SPOTS WITH LAWN CHAIRS--SOUNDS LIKE A GRAVEYARD YAWNING TO LIFE...

COFFIN LIDS UNHINGED, DIRT SLUFFED OFF, SKELETONS CLICKING THEIR JOINTS AND READYING TO DANCE.
IF YOU SAY I NEED TO MAKE SOME FRIENDS ONE MORE TIME, I SWEAR TO GOD I'LL DRINK DRANO OR NOSE-DIVE OFF A SKYSCRAPER.
I CAN'T HELP WHO I AM, OKAY? IT'S JUST THE WAY I'M HARD-WIRED.
I GOT AN IDEA.
YOU'RE NOT LISTENING TO ME. LISTEN TO ME.
IT'S HALLOWEEN. AND ON HALLOWEEN YOU PRETEND TO BE SOMETHING ELSE.
EVERYONE THINKS WE SUCK. SO LET'S FORGET WHO WE ARE FOR A LITTLE WHILE.

THERE IS A SMALL FARM OUTSIDE OF SEATTLE...
...OWNED BY A MAN NAMED TOMMY MALTMAN.
HE HAS A CHICKEN COOP, FOUR GOATS, A VEGETABLE PATCH, FRUIT TREES.
AND A BARN.
INSIDE THE BARN THERE ARE NO COWS OR HORSES.
THERE ARE PUPPETS.
MALTMAN IS FAMOUS FOR THEM. GIGANTIC PUPPETS.
MADE OF WOOD AND CLOTH AND PAPIER MÂCHÉ. SOME OF WHICH TAKE THREE OR MORE PEOPLE TO OPERATE.

HE BUILDS THEM FOR THEATERS AND PARADES.
OR AT LEAST HE USED TO.
TOMMY MALTMAN WON'T BE MAKING ANY MORE PUPPETS.
PEOPLE TALK ABOUT LUKOS AS IF IT MADE US LESSER.
BUT IT MAKES US MORE. AN ENHANCEMENT. THE ULTIMATE PREDATORY SYMBIOSIS.
I AM MAN, AND I AM WOLF!

THERE HAVE BEEN FEWER WARG ATTACKS THAN SHARK ATTACKS OVER THE PAST SIX MONTHS.
THE MONTHLY DOSES OF LUKOTREX REDUCE US TO MEWLING INVALIDS. AND NOW THEY'RE LEAKING OUR *NAMES* ONLINE? MAKING US *TARGETS?*
THEY HAVE NO REASON TO FEAR US, BUT THEY DO.
LET'S *JUSTIFY* THEIR FEARS.
LET'S CAST OFF THE CHOKE CHAIN AND THE MUZZLE.
LET'S *BITE* OUR *MASTERS!*
THEY SAY WE'RE DANGEROUS--*LET'S BE DANGEROUS!*
BE PROUD OF WHO YOU ARE!

EMI ASKED WHAT WOULD WE WEAR TO THE PARADE.
THEN WE LAUGHED.
THE ANSWER WAS OBVIOUS.
DON'T LOOK NOW.
DUDE! LOVE THE COSTUME!
Uh... YOU TOO.

SO--BACK TO WHAT YOU WERE SAYING EFORE. ARE YOU EELING GUILTY OUT THIS WHOLE WHITE SAVIOR THING?
I DON'T KNOW. IT'S JUST THIS GIRL. SHE BASICALLY SAID I WAS PRIVILEGED JERKOFF...
SOUNDS LIKE A PRETTY ACCURATE SYNONYM FOR BILLIONAIRE PLAYBOY.
HEY!
WHAT'S THE MATTER? DON'T LIKE TO SHARE, YOU SELFISH ONE-PERCENTER?
I'M JUST MESSING WITH YOU.
CLEAR OUT OF THE STREET, EVERYBODY!
MIDNIGHT PARADE'S COMING!

FOR MOST, ONE NIGHT A YEAR IS ENOUGH.
FOR ME, THE PROBLEM IS CHRONIC.
I LIVE IN A CONSTANT STATE OF SOMEONE ELSE-NESS.
MIDNIGHT PARADE

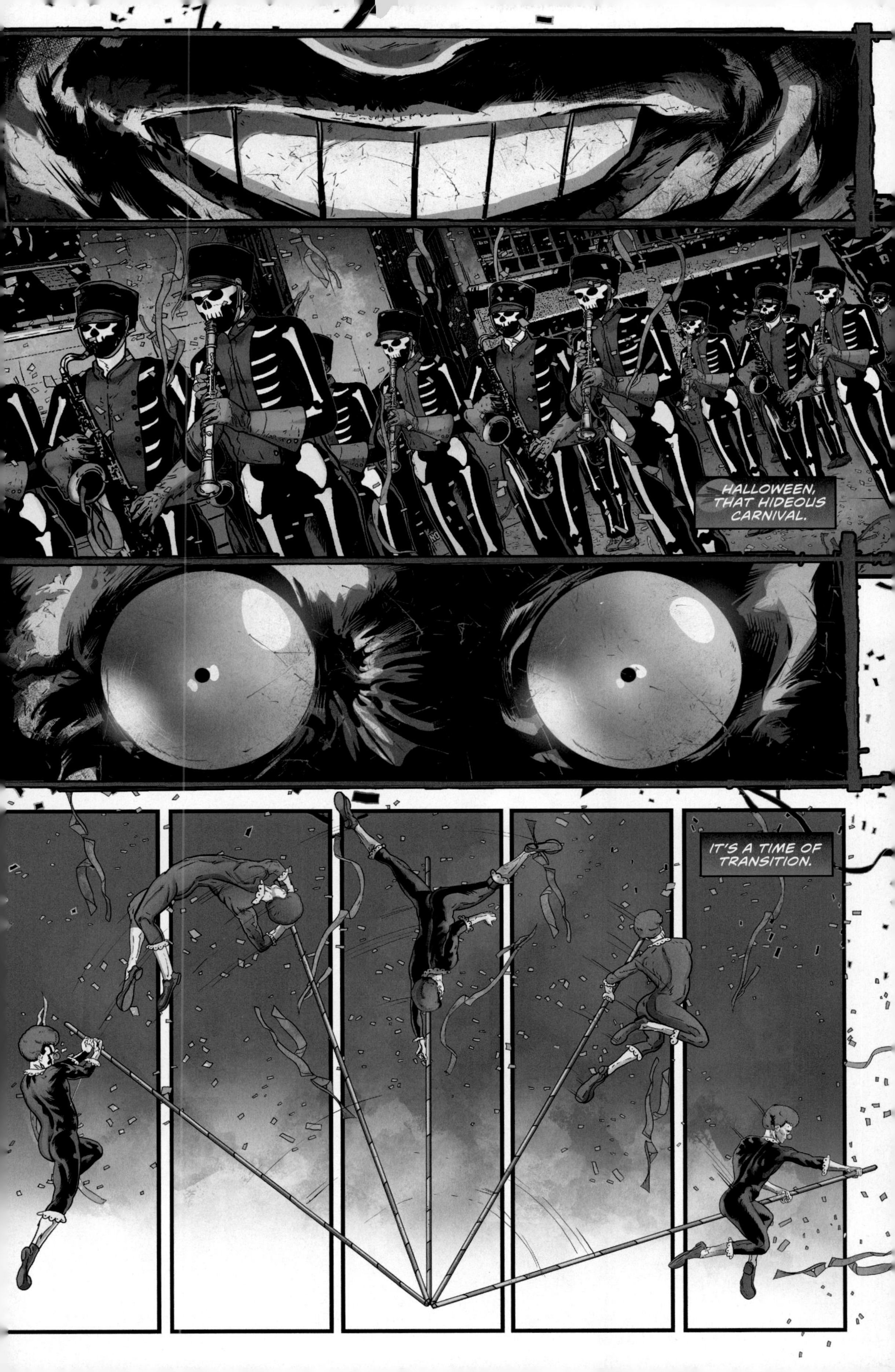
HALLOWEEN, THAT HIDEOUS CARNIVAL.
IT'S A TIME OF TRANSITION.

WHEN THE DARKER TIME OF THE YEAR BEGINS.
BE READY.
WHAT IS IT, GEORGE?
HAARRRRRRRR

THE WHITE VAN...
...GOT YOU.
WARG
HIGHWAY TO...!

EVERYBODY'S HERE. EVERYBODY'S SMILING.
EVERYBODY'S WAITING FOR SOMETHING SWEET. EVERYBODY'S IN FOR A SURPRISE.
NO TREATS, ONLY TRICKS TONIGHT.
IS THIS PART OF THE HALLOWEEN SHOW, DADDY?
I GUESS IT MUST BE.

DON'T KILL!
BITE!
BITE THEM ALL!
BLAM
BITE THEM ALL! SPREAD THE INFECTION!

THEY DON'T WANT US TO BE THEIR EQUALS. SO WE'LL MAKE THEM OURS.
WHAT'S HAPPENING?
TERROR!
IT'S A TERRORIST ATTACK!

OUR BODIES ARE A CAGE.
THERE IS A WILDNESS IN ALL OF US.
FOLLOW ME, SOLDIERS!
MOST PEOPLE CONTENTEDLY PEEK OUT OF THE BARS.
LET'S PUT THESE DOGS TO SLEEP!
OTHERS TEST THEM WITH A SHAKE.
AND SOME BREAK THROUGH ENTIRELY.
I DON'T KNOW WHO THE BAD GUYS ARE!
ANYBODY WHO'S NOT RUNNING.

SHE'S BEEN BITTEN?
YES. PLEASE HELP US.
SHE'S NO LONGER YOUR DAUGHTER, SIR. IT'S BETTER TO PUT HER OUT OF HER MIS--
THE NEXT ONE GOES IN YOUR EYE.

PFIT
PFIT
PFIT
WHEEEEEEEEEEEEZE
THWAP

YOU MADE ME FEEL SO SMALL AND WORTHLESS.
NO. PLEASE. I DIDN'T DO ANYTHING.
GRRRRRRRR

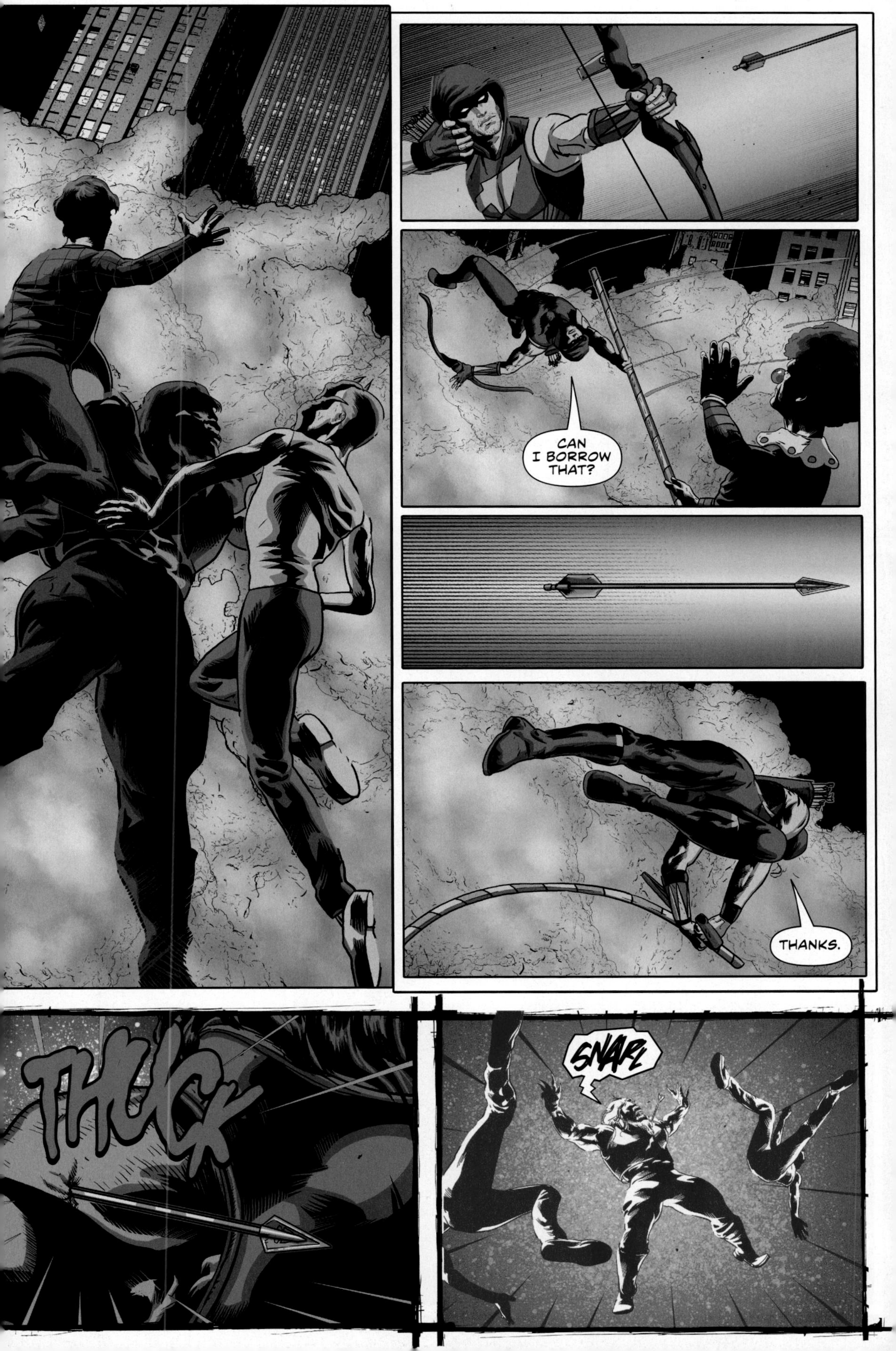
CAN I BORROW THAT?
THANKS.
THUCK
SNARL

WHO?
CRACK

BLAM
I WAS AIMING FOR YOUR MOUTH, MUTT. THIS TIME I WON'T MISS.
SHA-SHUNK

DON'T! THIS MAN NEEDS TO BE DETAINED AND QUESTIONED.
HE'S NOT A MAN.
GET OUT OF THE WAY OR I'LL--
THOK
THOK
THOK
SOME MONSTERS ARE HAIRY ON THE INSIDE.

IT'S OVER.
NO. IT'S NOT.
MIDNIGHT PARADE
BENJAMIN PERCY script • SZYMON KUDRANSKI art
storytellers
GABE ELTAEB colorist ROB LEIGH letterer TOMMY LEE EDWARDS cover
BRIAN CUNNINGHAM group editor HARVEY RICHARDS editor

SZYMON KUDRANSKI -15

EVERY NIGHT I WAKE UP SCREAMING.
AND FOR A MOMENT, I'M LOST BETWEEN ORLDS, UNCERTAIN WHO, WHERE, WHEN I AM.
MARROCK MIGHT BE CAGED IN A SUPERMAX, FACING THIRTY CHARGES FOR HIS ATTACK ON THE MIDNIGHT PARADE...

...BUT HE AND HIS BERSERKERS ROAM FREE IN MY DREAMS.
HE SEATTLE TI
HEARING TERROR AT TE
By Andrew Scott
It was a hellish scene in downtown Seattle, witnesses said during the preliminary hearing of Dolph Marrock. The pavement was blood-splattered and littered with torn-off limbs. Eyes burned from the smell of burned hair and gunsmoke.
I CAN STILL FEEL HIS TEETH.
BUT I FEEL FAR FROM NORMAL.
EEEEEEEEEEEEAAAAAAAAHHHH!
DID YOU HEAR THAT?
OR MAYBE IT WAS NOTHING.
MY OWN SCREAM CYCLING BACK TO ME.

WINTER CRUCIBLE
SOME PEOPLE GO TO CHURCH TO PRAY, ASK QUESTIONS, FIGURE THINGS OUT.
THIS IS MY CHURCH. THE WHITE-RAFTERED MOUNTAINS OF THE RAINIER WILDERNESS, WHERE, FOR THREE GENERATIONS, MY FAMILY HAS OWNED LAND.
CHIME
STORYTELLERS
BENJAMIN PERCY script
PATRICK ZIRCHER art
GABE ELTAEB colorist
ROB LEIGH letterer
SZYMON KUDRANSKI cover
CULLY HAMNER adult coloring book variant cover
BRIAN CUNNINGHAM group editor
HARVEY RICHARDS editor
EMI KNOWS I'M HIDING SOMETHING.
Home soon?
I miss ur constant nagging.
w/o guidance I'll prolly
rob a
let some
SHE THINKS SOMETHING'S WRONG.

TRUTH IS, I'VE NEVER FELT BETTER.
STRONGER. WILDER. FULLER.
MORE THAN A MAN. ENERGY WELLING INSIDE ME, BEGGING TO BE BURNED OFF.
AREN'T YOU GOING TO LEND ME A PAW?
RIGHT ABOUT HERE IS WHERE WE SAW THAT BUCK TWO DAYS AGO.
I CAN'T FLY, CAN'T BREATHE UNDERWATER, DEFLECT BULLETS, CONTROL THE WEATHER, THROW FIRE.
FIRST WORLD PROBLEMS. THAT'S WHAT EMI WOULD SAY.
BUT YOU PUT ME IN A LINEUP WITH THE JUSTICE LEAGUE-- OR EVEN SOME OF THE GUTTER-LEVEL BADDIES I'VE FACED...
...AND I CAN'T HELP BUT FEEL INADEQUATE, UNEXCEPTIONAL, COMPARATIVELY DISABLED.

NOW--WITH THE LUKOS INFECTION COURSING THROUGH ME, A DISEASE THAT MAKES ME BOTH WOLF AND MAN--MY SENSES ARE JACKED.
I CAN SMELL AND SEE AND HEAR AND FEEL EVERYTHING AS IF IT WERE TEN TIMES THE SIZE.
THE WHISK OF AN OWL'S WING, THE SIGH OF A BRANCH UNSHOULDERING SNOW.
WHAT THE HELL?
SAP RIDES THE BREEZE. BERRIES BLAZE ON BUSHES. TRACKS SPRING FROM THE GROUND.
SNAP
KRACK

OH NO YOU DON'T.
IF THIS IS WHAT IT MEANS TO BE A WARG...

LUNCH IS ON ME!
...THEN I'M IN NO RUSH TO DISCOVER A CURE.

THIS IS A NICE TREAT, A GOOD SURPRISE. THANK YOU, OLIVER.

LEAST I CAN DO, NORTON.
WORLD'S BEST DAD
THANKS FOR ALL YOUR HELP OVER THE YEARS. LOOKING AFTER MY FAMILY'S LAND.
YOU'VE THANKED ME PLENTY. I CLEAN GUTTERS, PLUG LEAKS, MEND FENCES, CHASE AWAY TRESPASSERS, AND YOU PAY ME AS IF I HAD A MEDICAL DEGREE.
WHERE ARE YOUR GLASSES?
SLIPPED ON THE ICE. BROKE MY GLASSES.
SEE YOU'RE NURSING AN INJURY, TOO. COME TO THINK OF IT, I'VE NEVER SEEN YOU UNBRUISED, UNBROKEN.
ROUGH WORK, BEING A C.E.O.
MY MEMORY MUST BE GOING. I THOUGHT YOU TOOK YOUR MEAT MEDIUM WELL?
THESE DAYS, I'VE GOT A TASTE FOR RARE.

WORLD'S BEST DAD
I WAS SORRY TO HEAR ABOUT YOUR SON.
YES... HE GOT SICK... AND...
I'M SORRY.
DAMN.
WHAT'S THE MATTER?
SOMETHING GOT INTO THE DEER. I SHOULD HAVE FINISHED BUTCHERING IT.
THAT REMINDS ME. DID YOU HEAR ANYTHING THE OTHER NIGHT? A SCREAMING?
NO. NOTHING LIKE THAT.
MAYBE IT'S WOLVES. MAYBE IT'S THE WIND.
YEAH, MAYBE.

NOT GOING TO BE ABLE TO MAKE IT, BRODERICK.
THAT'S *UFF* NOT AN OPTION.
THEY'RE FLYING IN FROM SEOUL, AND THEY'RE READY TO MAKE AN OFFER ON THE CARBON NANOTUBE BATTERY.
THIS WOULD *ARGH!* PUT THE BATTERY INTO CARS, PHONES, WATCHES, WITHIN A YEAR. AND HOMES WITHIN FIVE.
THIS IS THE PLATFORM QUEEN INDUSTRIES HAS BEEN WAITING FOR.
SNAP
ARE YOU OKAY? YOU SOUND--
I'M FINE. FOCUS ON YOU.
CAN'T YOU HANDLE THIS WITHOUT ME? I'M WORKING MY WAY THROUGH SOME... TROUBLES.
WE ALL HAVE TROUBLES, OLIVER. SOME OF US JUST DO A BETTER JOB OF MANAGING THEM PRIVATELY. BE HERE.
YOU'VE BEEN VERY, VERY BAD.

WHAT THE--
SOMETHING'S OUT THERE.
MY FATHER USED TO TELL ME CAMPFIRE STORIES ABOUT A WILD MAN WHO LIVED IN THE WOODS.
COVERED IN FUR. WITH LONG YELLOW CLAWS AND LONG YELLOW TEETH.

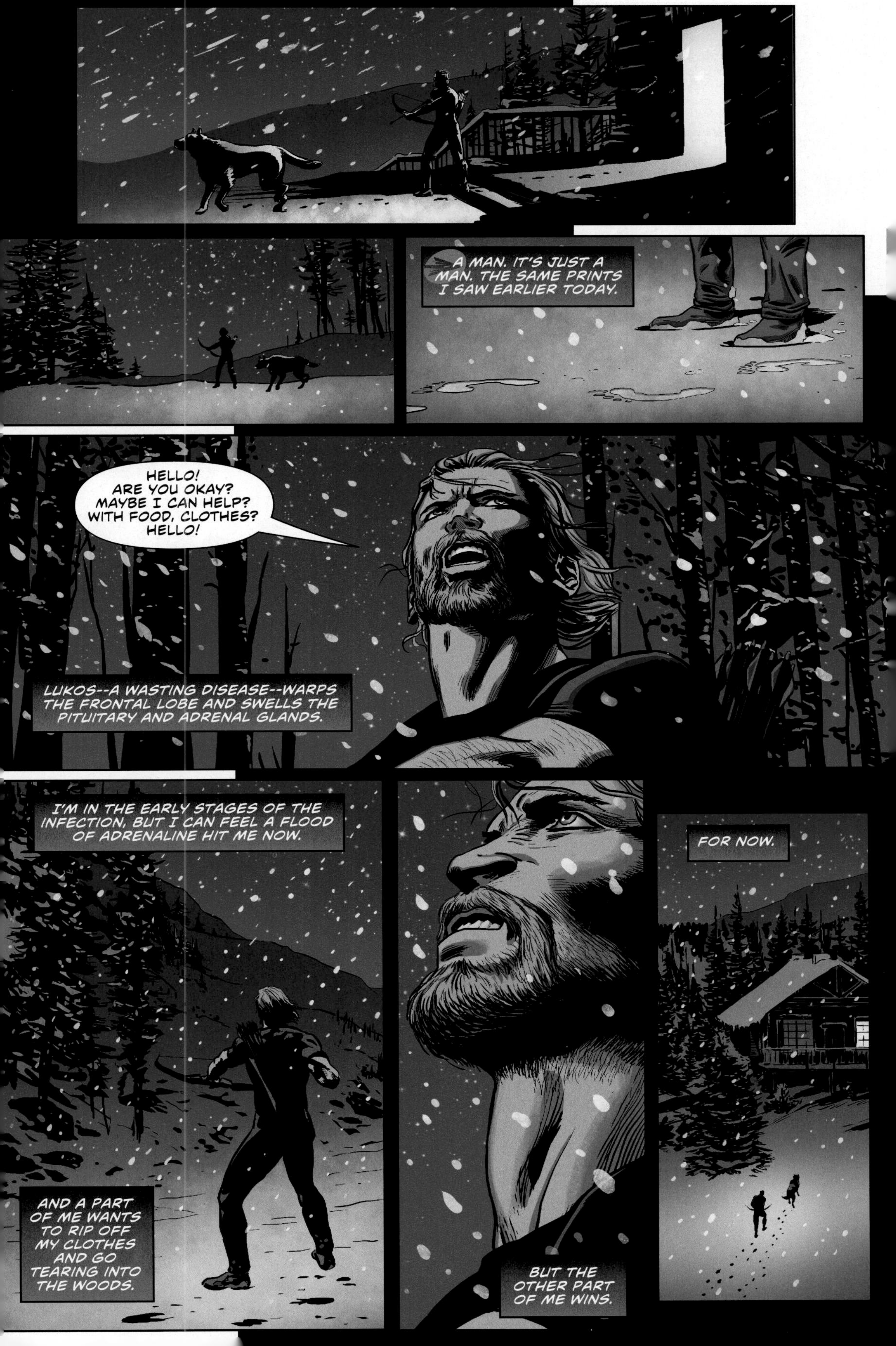
A MAN. IT'S JUST A MAN. THE SAME PRINTS I SAW EARLIER TODAY.
HELLO! ARE YOU OKAY? MAYBE I CAN HELP? WITH FOOD, CLOTHES? HELLO!
LUKOS--A WASTING DISEASE--WARPS THE FRONTAL LOBE AND SWELLS THE PITUITARY AND ADRENAL GLANDS.
I'M IN THE EARLY STAGES OF THE INFECTION, BUT I CAN FEEL A FLOOD OF ADRENALINE HIT ME NOW.
AND A PART OF ME WANTS TO RIP OFF MY CLOTHES AND GO TEARING INTO THE WOODS.
BUT THE OTHER PART OF ME WINS.
FOR NOW.

WHAT IS IT, GEORGE? YOU SMELL SOMETHING?
TEN INCHES FELL LAST NIGHT.
HUFF
TEN MORE ARE EXPECTED TO FALL BEFORE THE SKIES CLEAR.
WHATEVER, WHOEVER IS OUT HERE...
...I DON'T KNOW IF I'M HERE TO SAVE THEM OR HUNT THEM.
RRRRRRRRRRRRRRR
WHOA, WHOA, WHOA-- PLEASE DON'T SHOOT.
THIS IS PRIVATE LAND. WHAT ARE YOU DOING HERE?
WE'RE LOST. WE WERE SNOW CAMPING AND OUR G.P.S. WENT DEAD. WE'RE JUST TRYING TO GET TO OUR CAR.

THERE YOU GO. TWO DOUBLE As.
THANK YOU SO MUCH.
BETTER HURRY. STORM'S GOING TO GET WORSE BEFORE IT GETS BETTER.
LET'S GO, GEORGE.
GEORGE?
GEORGE!
SMELLS LIKE DEATH.
WHAT IS THIS PLACE? A PRISON OR A LAIR?
I KNOW WHO TO ASK.
NORTON...

MY MUSCLES BURN AND MY LUNGS FEEL CLAWED OUT, BUT I DON'T PAUSE UNTIL WE GET TO HIS CABIN.
TOO LATE.
NORTON, WHERE ARE YOU?
NORTON! WHAT HAPPENED?
I COULDN'T SEE. I COULDN'T SEE.
UuuUGghh
I FOUND THEM. YOUR GLASSES.
NO. I MEAN I COULDN'T SEE HIM. WHAT HE HAD BECOME.
WHAT ARE YOU TALKING ABOUT?
MY SON. I *LIED*. HE'S *NOT* DEAD. HE'S SICK.
HE'S *INFECTED*. HE WAS BITTEN BY ONE OF THE INFECTED WOLVES.
HE REFUSED TO REPORT THE BITE, TO MEDICATE. SAID HE LIKED THE INFECTION.
BUT THEN IT TOOK HIM OVER. THE WOLF TOOK OVER.
BUT THEN HE GOT LOOSE. HE'S OUT THERE.
AND HE'S HUNGRY.

JOSH...
TIME FOR A WATER BREAK? SOUNDS GOOD.
I THOUGHT I SAW--I GUESS IT WAS NOTHING.
ISN'T IT BEAUTIFUL?
I'M STARTING TO THINK GETTING LOST IS THE BEST THING THAT COULD HAVE HAPPENED TO US.

THE SYMPTOMS OF LUKOS ARE PROVOKED BY FEAR, ANGER, EXHAUSTION, HUNGER.
WHEN IT TAKES HOLD OF ME, IT'S LIKE SEX IN MY VEINS, LIKE A FULL MOON IN MY HEART, A HEIGHTENING, AN UNRAVELING.
I CAN SEE WHY SOME EMBRACE THE DISEASE AND SAY IT IS LESS AN INFECTION AND MORE A TRANSCENDENT IDENTITY.
EEEEEAAHH!
HELP! SOMEBODY HELP!

GRRRRRR
I DON'T NEED AN ARROW.
YELP
I AM AN ARROW.

CRACK

I CAN SEE HIM NOW.
I CAN SEE THIS NEEDS TO END.
IT'S ALL RIGHT. EVERYTHING'S GOING TO BE ALL RIGHT.
OR AT LEAST THAT'S WHAT I THINK I SAY.
GRAAAARRRR
GET AWAY FROM US, YOU MONSTER! STAY AWAY!

I'VE LIVED SUCH A PRIVILEGED LIFE.
AT FIRST I THOUGHT LUKOS WAS A WAY TO ENHANCE THAT PRIVILEGE-- FOR ME TO BE EXCEPTIONAL.
NOW I UNDERSTAND IT'S A NECESSARY WAY TO BRING ME DOWN.
I'VE COMMITTED MYSELF TO HELPING THOSE WHO ARE MARGINALIZED...
...WITHOUT TRULY KNOWING WHAT IT MEANS TO BE DISADVANTAGED, WRONGED, VIEWED AS OTHER.
MAYBE THIS IS A WAY TO BECOME A BETTER HERO AND PERSON, TO LEARN EMPATHY.
MAYBE LUKOS IS THE DIAGNOSIS AND THE CURE.

PRIMAL INSTINCTS
IN 1925, THE KU KLUX KLAN HAD OVER FIVE MILLION MEMBERS, MAKING IT THE LARGEST FRATERNAL ORGANIZATION IN THE COUNTRY.
MOST PEOPLE WOULD SAY WE'VE COME A LONG WAY.
NOT ME.
THERE'S PLENTY OF HATE IN THE AIR.
POLICE
POLICE
THE KING COUNTY DISTRICT COURT HOUSE.
storytellers: BENJAMIN PERCY script • SZYMON KUDRANSKI art
GABE ELTAEB colorist • ROB LEIGH letterer • SZYMON KUDRANSKI cover
NEAL ADAMS, JIM LEE and ALEX SINCLAIR variant cover
BRIAN CUNNINGHAM group editor • HARVEY RICHARDS editor
THANK YOU! WE LOVE YOU! GOD LOVES YOU!
CLAP CLAP WOO! CLAP CLAP WOO! CLAP
WE'RE GOING TO CONTINUE TO DO HIS GOOD WORK BY RIDDING THIS WORLD OF A PESTILENCE.
IF THE ATTACKS AT THE MIDNIGHT PARADE TAUGHT U ANYTHING, IT IS THI NO ONE IS SAFE FRO THE *WARGS.*

SO MARROCK REMAINS IN SOLITARY CONFINEMENT, WHILE THE PATRIOTS WALK FREE?
THIS IS BULL, CHIEF WESTBERG.
THE CASE AGAINST THEM ISN'T EVEN MAKING IT OUT OF DISTRICT COURT?
THIS IS OUT OF MY HANDS, MISTER QUEEN.
POLICE
POLICE
I ♥ PATRIOTS
GOD HATES WARG
"THE PATRIOTS KILLED PEOPLE."
"THEY STOPPED A TERRORIST ATTACK. MOST WOULD SAY THEY SAVED LIVES."
THIS IS STATE-SANCTIONED VIOLENCE.
YOU HAVE EFFECTIVELY LEGALIZED A LYNCH MOB.
WHAT'S GOTTEN INTO YOU? WHY DO YOU CARE SO MUCH ANYWAY?
BECAUSE I'VE GOT A DOG IN THIS FIGHT.

QUEEN INDUSTRIES HIRES ONLY THE TOP RESEARCHERS, OUTBIDDING SILICON VALLEY IN ORDER TO STEAL AWAY THE TOP TALENT FROM M.I.T. AND STANFORD.
WE ARE IMPRESSED AND GRATEFUL THAT YOU WOULD CONSIDER JEON-WI AS A PARTNER COMPANY.
WE'VE BEEN DEVELOPING THE CARBON NANOTUBES FOR YEARS. YOUR COMPANY OFFERS THE IDEAL PLATFORM.
YOU'RE A MILLION MILES AWAY, OLIVER. I NEED YOU HERE.
DID YOU EVEN SHOWER? DOES THIS MEAN ANYTHING TO YOU?
I KNOW THOSE TATTOOS.
KRAKEN.
A KOREAN GANGSTER WHO RECENTLY TOOK CONTROL OF THE SEATTLE PORTS TO SMUGGLE DRUGS, WOMEN, WEAPONS.
HE'S REMAINED ON THE OTHER SIDE OF THE PACIFIC.
UNTIL NOW.

THIS MIGHT BE A FIVE HUNDRED DOLLAR DINNER, BUT THERE'S A BILLION DOLLARS ON THE LINE.
THE NANOTUBES ARE NOT A BATTERY, BUT A SUPERCAPACITOR THAT PUTS LITHIUM ENERGY TO SHAME.
AND ITS FIBROUS QUALITY HAS ALL SORTS OF POTENTIAL, SO THAT IT MIGHT BE WOVEN INTO CLOTHES, EVEN SKIN.
EXCUSE ME, GENTLEMEN.
BEFORE I WAS BITTEN AND INFECTED WITH LUKOS, I COULD HAVE CONTROLLED MYSELF.
BEEN A BUSINESSMAN NOW, A HERO LATER.
BUT I AM LOSING CONTROL OF MY MANY SELVES.
IT'S DIFFICULT TO MAINTAIN CONTROL...

...WHEN YOU'VE GOT WOLVES CRASHING THROUGH YOUR VEINS.
THE PRINTING PRESS. THE SPINNING JENNY. THE COMBUSTIBLE ENGINE. THE INTEL PROCESSOR.
KRASH
EVERY NOW AND THEN SOMETHING COMES ALONG AND CHANGES EVERYTHING. I THINK THESE NANOTUBES WILL BE...
...EVOLUTIONARY.

TRANSFORMATIVE.
I FEEL LIKE MY SKIN IS GOING TO SPLIT, LIKE IT CAN'T CONTAIN THE PRIMAL ENERGY INSIDE ME.

BLAT
BLAT
BLAT
BLAT
BLAT

GO, GO, GO!
DON'T STOP! RUN HIM DOWN!

SNARL
THWAP
WHAT HIT ME?
TRANQ ARROW?!
EMIKO!
I'M... FADING...

SO, SO, SO, SO DUMB. D-U-M DUMB.
DID YOU REALLY THINK I WOULDN'T FIND OUT?
WHY DIDN'T YOU TELL ME THAT MARROCK BIT YOU?
WHY DIDN'T YOU TELL ME YOU WERE A WARG?
GREEN ARROW HQ.

LET ME OUT, EMI! LET ME OUT RIGHT NOW OR I'LL--
OR YOU'LL WHAT? TAKE A BITE OUT OF ME?
YOU'RE NOT GOING ANYWHERE.
WHAT IS THAT? WHAT ARE YOU DOING?
30 CC'S OF LUKONEX. I WANT MY BROTHER BACK.
YOU DON'T UNDERSTAND. I LIKE IT. IT'S MADE ME SPECIAL, POWERFUL.
YOU'RE OUT OF CONTROL. YOU'RE LIKE A DOG CHASING AFTER EVERY BAD SMELL.
IT'S NOT A DISEASE. IT'S ME NOW. IT'S WHO I AM!
YOU KNOW, EVERY NOW AND THEN I ACTUALLY LEARN SOMETHING AT THAT RIDICULOUS DAY CARE CENTER YOU MAKE ME GO TO, DARK WATER HIGH SCHOOL.
WE READ A PRETTY GOOD BOOK THE OTHER DAY.
IT SAID IF A MAN LOSES A LEG OR AN EYE, HE KNOWS IT. BUT IF HE LOSES HIMSELF, HE CAN'T KNOW...
...BECAUSE HE'S NO LONGER THERE TO REALIZE IT.
SO I'M HERE TO TELL YOU, OLLIE. YOU'VE LOST YOURSELF.

W CHRISTIAN CHURCH AND OUTREACH CENTER.
OUR TIME IS NOW, FRIENDS AND BRETHREN.
nccoc new christian ...ch and ...center
DONORS:
John and Fred Coke 500k
Chicken Fill Restaurants 100k
Guns and God 125k
The Moral Project 5k
BUSINESS ITEMS
1. Hire support staff
2. Establish website and membership
3. Online campaign
4. Seek political
ACTION ITEMS
1. Demand public Warg registry
2. Proliferate hospital records of infected
3. Vandalism, picketing, bombing
4. Assassinations
FROM PRIVATE AND BUSINESS DONORS ALL OVER THE COUNTRY, WE'VE RECEIVED OVER A MILLION DOLLARS TO FUND OUR EFFORTS.
THE TROUBLE IS, THERE HAVE BEEN RUMORS, BUT NO VERIFIABLE WARG ATTACKS SINCE THE MIDNIGHT PARADE.
AND LIBERAL PANTYWAIST HUMAN RIGHTS ORGANIZATIONS ARE ALREADY CLOSING IN, TRYING TO PROTECT THE INFECTED.
PROTECT HEM? THAT'S SANE. WHO'S GOING TO PROTECT THE REST OF US?
WE ARE.
AND TO KEEP THIS GROUNDSWELL OF SUPPORT GOING, WE NEED TO MAKE A MOVE. TONIGHT.

"PUT ON YOUR MASKS.
"IT'S TIME TO LET THE DOG OUT OF HIS KENNEL.
WASHINGTON STATE PENITENTIARY. WALLA WALLA.
"DOLPH MARROCK IS IN SOLITARY CONFINEMENT FOR TWENTY-THREE HOURS EVERY DAY.
"THE TWENTY-FOURTH HOUR HE SPENDS OUTSIDE IN AN OPEN CELL BARELY BIG ENOUGH FOR HIM TO PACE.
"THIS TAKES PLACE AT EXACTLY 9 PM EVERY NIGHT."
ALL RIGHT, MARROCK. YOU KNOW THE ROUTINE. HANDS THROUGH THE SLOTS.

"WHICH IS THE EXACT MOMENT MY INSIDE CONTACT--BRIBED WITH OUR HEALTHY RESERVES OF CASH--WILL CUT THE POWER."
WHAT THE...
"THE EMERGENCY LIGHTS WILL FLASH RED FOR ONE MINUTE."
NO!
GAAAAAA!
13

"OUTSIDE, THE GUARDS' ATTENTION WILL BE ELSEWHERE.
BA-BOOM
"MAYBE MARROCK WILL GET OUT, MAYBE HE WON'T.
RUM-RUM-RUM-RUM-RUM
SCREEEEEEEE

"BUT BY THE TIME THE GENERATORS BRING THE POWER BACK ONLINE...
"...OUR RABID DOG WILL HAVE CREATED ENOUGH TERROR TO FILL TWO WEEKS OF HEADLINES."
WOOF
BARK
YELP

FOUND
OMETHING.
"AND WE'LL MAKE SURE THEY KNOW WHO TO BLAME.
"WHO TO FEAR, WHO TO PUNISH."
JUST AS THEY'LL KNOW WHO TO TURN TO FOR HELP.

THAT LUKONEX MAKES ME FEEL LIKE HELL.
THINK OF IT LIKE A CHOKE COLLAR. A NECESSARY RESTRAINT.
THANKS FOR TAKING CARE OF ME.
WHEN I WAS LYING THERE, I COULDN'T HELP BUT THINK OF THIS TIME, A THOUSAND YEARS AGO, WHEN I HAD TO STAY HOME SICK.
I KEPT ASKING MY MOTHER TO READ THIS PICTURE BOOK TO ME OVER AND OVER AGAIN. IT WAS ABOUT CONSTELLATIONS.
EVERY ANIMAL SAW THE SAME STARS DIFFERENTLY. THE CHICKE SAW A HENHOUSE, THE BEA SAW A RIVER FULL OF SALM THAT KIND OF THING. SHE KE ASKING ME IF I UNDERSTO WHAT IT MEANT.
AND I DO. FOR THE FIRST TIME, I FEEL LIKE I'M SEEING A NEW CONSTELLATION, SEEING THE WORLD FROM A DISADVANTAGED POINT OF VIEW.
IT'S GIVING ME ANOTHER REASON, MAYBE A BETTER REASON, TO FIGHT.
LOOK, CAPTAIN EMPATHY, I'M ALL FOR PRIVILEGED JERK-OFFS GETTING KNOCKED OFF THEIR HIGH HORSES.
BUT WE NEED TO FIND A CURE BEFORE YOU LOSE YOUR SENSE OF SELF ENTIRELY.

EMI?
WHAT IS IT, FYFF?
HOT OFF THE WIRE. MARROCK HAS ESCAPED THE SUPERMAX.
DOZENS ARE DEAD. SOUNDS LIKE HE HAD HELP.
SUIT UP.
A WAR IS BREWING.
AND NEITHER SIDE IS WORTH FIGHTING FOR.

GABE
ELTAEB

ENNYTOWN, SEATTLE.
BLOOD BANK
BLOOD BANK
Blood for Cash
EZ Payday
O NEGATIVE? BE POSITIVE.
U GIVE BLOOD, WE G1VE $.
BLOOD CURE
storytellers:
BENJAMIN PERCY script · SZYMON KUDRANSKI art
GABE ELTAEB colorist · ROB LEIGH letterer
ATRICK ZIRCHER with GABE ELTAEB cover · AARON KUDER with TOMEU MOREY variant cover
BRIAN CUNNINGHAM group editor
HARVEY RICHARDS editor
WHAT ARE YOU IN THE MOOD FOR, BIG GUY?
BLOOD.

GOOD EVENING. IS THIS YOUR FIRST TIME OR HAVE YOU DONATED BEFORE?
GIVEN PLENTY OF BLOOD. TAKEN SOME TOO.
DONOR APPLICATION
Blood Type
Address
IF YOU CAN JUST FILL OUT THIS FORM--
THIS QUESTION RIGHT HERE...
"HAVE YOU EVER BEEN DIAGNOSED WITH, OR HAVE YOU EVER BEEN IN CONTACT WITH ANYONE WITH A CHRONIC OR ALIEN ILLNESS?"

DO I REALLY EED TO ANSWER THAT?
I NEED YOUR HELP, FRIEND. DO AS YOU'RE TOLD AND I WON'T MAKE A SNACK OF YOUR FACE.
"HANG UP THE CLOSED SIGN.
"UNLOCK THE DOOR TO THE DONATION ROOM.
"READY THE NEEDLES.
"BECAUSE I'VE GOT SOME NEW DONORS I WANT YOU TO MEET."

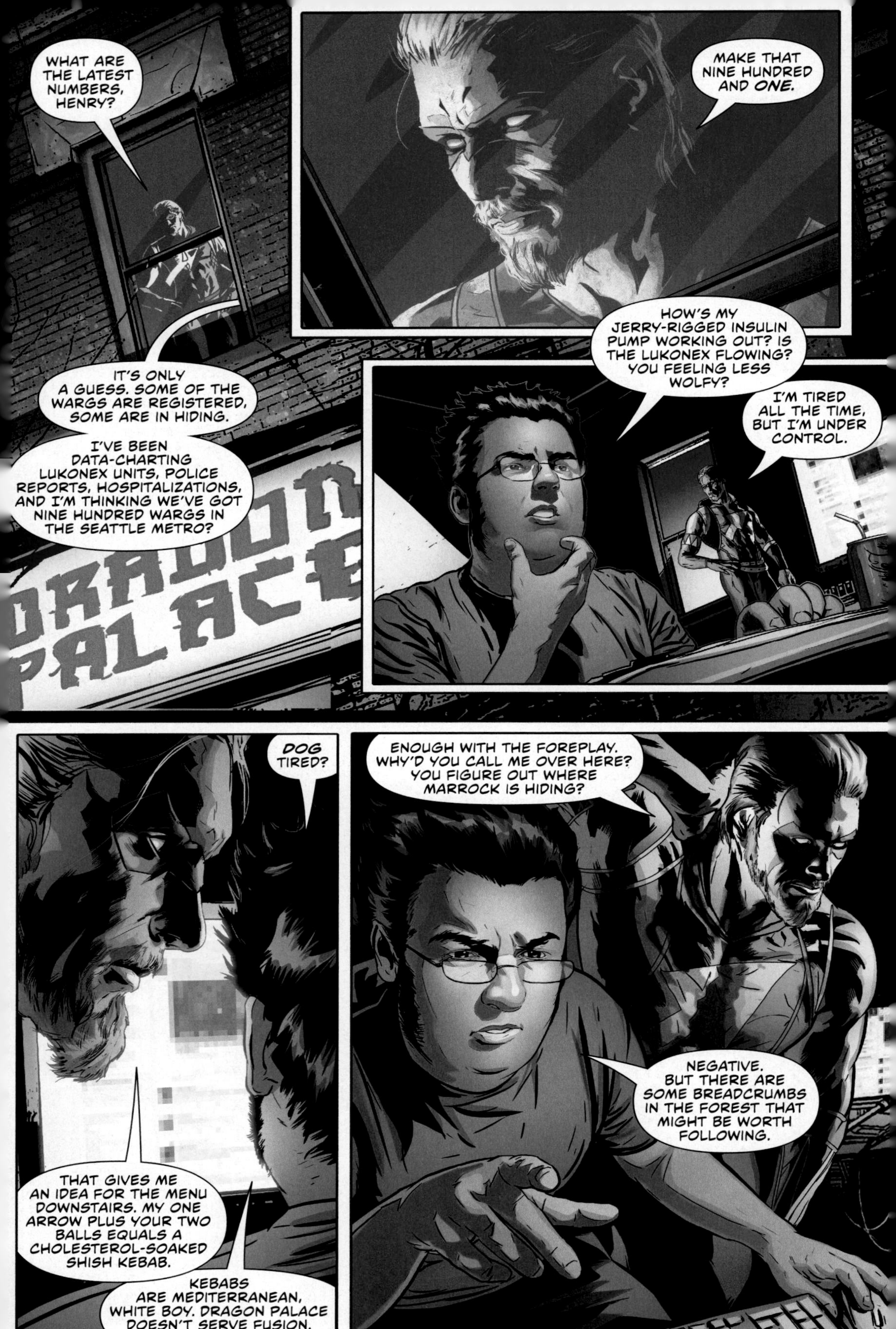
WHAT ARE THE LATEST NUMBERS, HENRY?
IT'S ONLY A GUESS. SOME OF THE WARGS ARE REGISTERED, SOME ARE IN HIDING.
I'VE BEEN DATA-CHARTING LUKONEX UNITS, POLICE REPORTS, HOSPITALIZATIONS, AND I'M THINKING WE'VE GOT NINE HUNDRED WARGS IN THE SEATTLE METRO?
DRAGON PALACE
MAKE THAT NINE HUNDRED AND *ONE*.
HOW'S MY JERRY-RIGGED INSULIN PUMP WORKING OUT? IS THE LUKONEX FLOWING? YOU FEELING LESS WOLFY?
I'M TIRED ALL THE TIME, BUT I'M UNDER CONTROL.
DOG TIRED?
THAT GIVES ME AN IDEA FOR THE MENU DOWNSTAIRS. MY ONE ARROW PLUS YOUR TWO BALLS EQUALS A CHOLESTEROL-SOAKED SHISH KEBAB.
KEBABS ARE MEDITERRANEAN, WHITE BOY. DRAGON PALACE DOESN'T SERVE FUSION.
ENOUGH WITH THE FOREPLAY. WHY'D YOU CALL ME OVER HERE? YOU FIGURE OUT WHERE MARROCK IS HIDING?
NEGATIVE. BUT THERE ARE SOME BREADCRUMBS IN THE FOREST THAT MIGHT BE WORTH FOLLOWING.

OS IS TRANSMITTED BY BLOOD OR
JAL CONTACT, RIGHT? WELL, NOT
ATTACKS HAVE BEEN REPORTED.
"AND--CORRECT ME IF I'M WRONG, ROMEO--BUT MOST PEOPLE ARE PRETTY GOOD ABOUT KEEPING IT WRAPPED THESE DAYS.
"IN OTHER WORDS, THE
MBERS DON'T ADD UP. HOW IS
THE INFECTION SPREADING?
BLOOD BANK
BLOOD BANK
EZ Payday
U GIVE BLOOD, WE GIVE $.
"I DID SOME DIGGING. SEVERAL NEWLY REGISTERED WARGS RECEIVED BLOOD TRANSFUSIONS OVER THE PAST WEEK.
"THERE'S A KIND OF BLOOD CRISIS GOING ON RIGHT NOW. NOT ENOUGH DONORS.
"SO THESE PAY-BY-THE-PINT CENTERS ARE POPPING UP ALL OVER THE PLACE. ENTICING PEOPLE TO OPEN UP THEIR VEINS.
"THE CENTERS PRICK AND BAG, TEST FOR DISEASE, THEN SELL TO DESPERATE HOSPITALS."
T I COULD
YOUR WHOLE
EAD IN MY
MOUTH.
YOU'VE MENTIONED THAT SEVERAL TIMES, MISTER MARROCK.
JUST A FRIENDLY REMINDER TO KEEP DOING AS YOU'RE TOLD.
KEEP SPREADING THE INFECTION. KEEP BATHING THIS CITY IN OUR BLOOD.

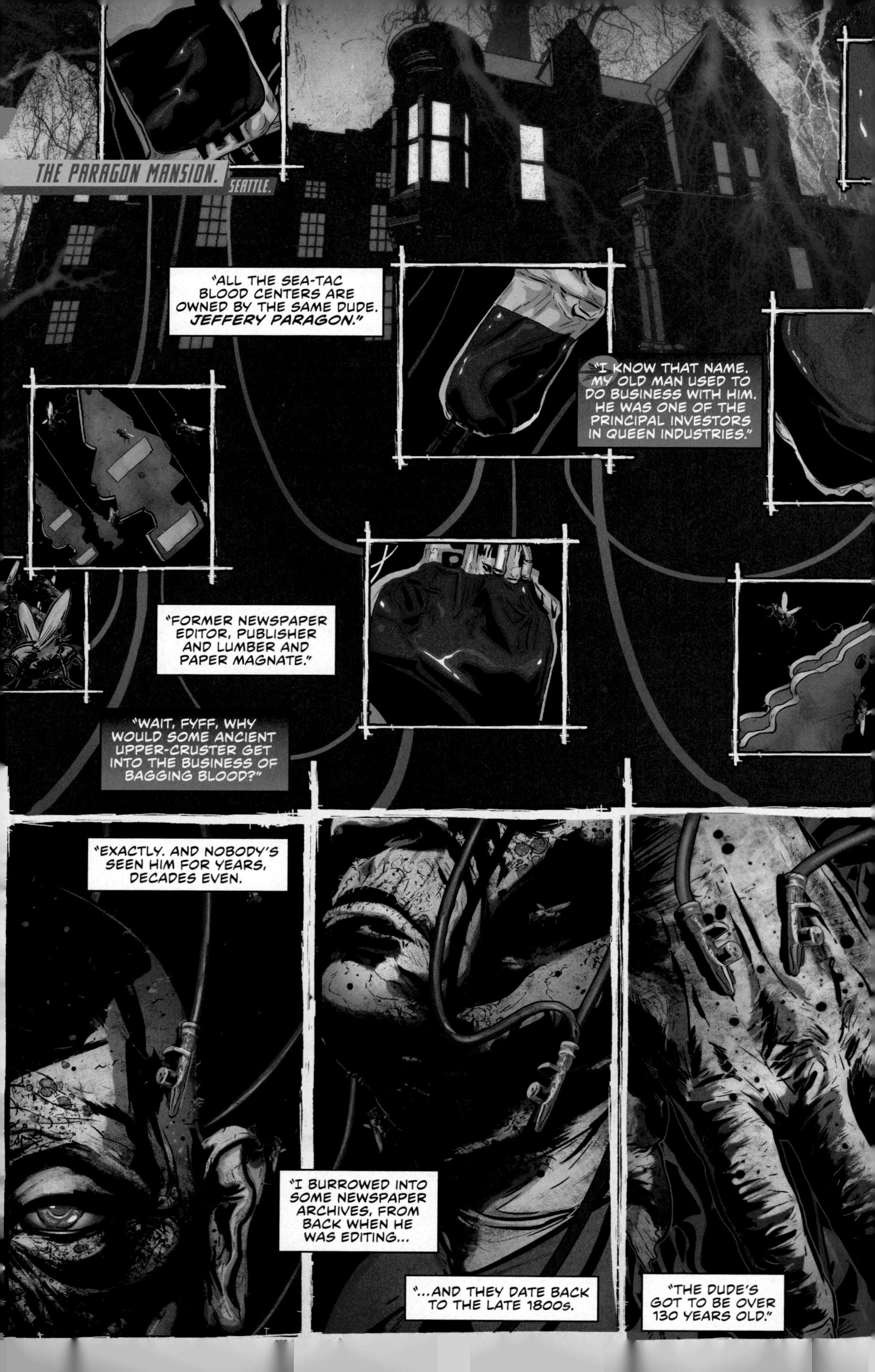
THE PARAGON MANSION.
SEATTLE.
"ALL THE SEA-TAC BLOOD CENTERS ARE OWNED BY THE SAME DUDE. JEFFERY PARAGON."
"I KNOW THAT NAME. MY OLD MAN USED TO DO BUSINESS WITH HIM. HE WAS ONE OF THE PRINCIPAL INVESTORS IN QUEEN INDUSTRIES."
"FORMER NEWSPAPER EDITOR, PUBLISHER AND LUMBER AND PAPER MAGNATE."
"WAIT, FYFF, WHY WOULD SOME ANCIENT UPPER-CRUSTER GET INTO THE BUSINESS OF BAGGING BLOOD?"
"EXACTLY. AND NOBODY'S SEEN HIM FOR YEARS, DECADES EVEN.
"I BURROWED INTO SOME NEWSPAPER ARCHIVES, FROM BACK WHEN HE WAS EDITING...
"...AND THEY DATE BACK TO THE LATE 1800s.
"THE DUDE'S GOT TO BE OVER 130 YEARS OLD."

"YOU THINK HE HAS SOMETHING TO DO WITH SPREADING THE INFECTION, FYFF?"
"NO. YES. I DON'T KNOW. BUT IT'S A LEAD WORTH CHASING."
HAVE YOU HEARD ANY NEWS FROM THE MERCENARY?
I'M AFRAID, SIR, THAT NORTH KOREA WAS A DEAD END.
DAMN HIM. DOESN'T HE KNOW HOW LITTLE TIME I HAVE? I COULD BE DEAD IN A WEEK.
SHALL I READY THE DAY'S THIRD TRANSFUSION, SIR?
PLEASE. I'M DESPERATELY THIRSTY TODAY.

I CAN'T HELP BUT IMAGINE YOUR EXERCISE BALL AS AN EGG. AN EGG YOU'RE SLOWLY WARMING TO HATCH SOMETHING TERRIBLE.
YOU'RE JUST JEALOUS OF MY RIPPED CORE.
I'LL CHECK OUT THE BLOOD CENTERS.
AND I'LL SEND A SCOUT TO THE PARAGO MANSION.
SCOUT?
REMEMBER AARON ZIMM'S PANOPTICON DRONES?
I'VE BEEN MESSIN AROUND WITH THE SCRAPS OF ONE. MODDING IT.
GREEN ARROW IS NOW IN THE SURVEILLANCE BUSINESS.
MEET OUR NEW PET DRONE.

BOLA QUARANTINE STATION. LIBERIA.
EVERY FEW MONTHS, THERE ARE WHISPERS...
...ABOUT A HEALER. A MAN CAPABLE OF MIRACLES.
GOT ANOTHER ONE!
HIS PARENTS ARE DEAD. AND I'M AFRAID HE'S SOON TO FOLLOW.
WE DON'T HAVE TIME FOR LOST CAUSES. WE'RE OVERWHELMED AS IT IS.
I'VE GOT HIM.
ON AN INDIAN RESERVATION IN OKLAHOMA, ON A TYPHOON-RAVAGED BEACH IN THAILAND.
IF THERE IS AN EARTHQUAKE, A HEAT WAVE, A FLOOD, A NUCLEAR MELTDOWN, HE'LL BE THERE. OR SO PEOPLE SAY.
IT'S GOING TO BE OKAY.
UNNNNNGH!
DOCTOR MIRACLE. THAT'S WHAT THEY CALL HIM.
STAY WITH ME.

SOME SAY DOCTOR MIRACLE IS A WOMAN. OTHERS, A MAN. OTHERS, AN ANGEL.
SOME SAY HE'S WISHFUL THINKING, A PIPE DREAM.
BUT ONE THING'S FOR SURE.
Huh?
IF DOCTOR MIRACLE DOES EXIST, HE DOESN'T WANT TO BE FOUND OUT.

FOR GOOD REASON.
THERE NOW.
BECAUSE PEOPLE WANT TO DESTROY WHATEVER IS DIFFERENT.
WITCH!
WHATEVER THEY DON'T UNDERSTAND.
I SAW, I SAW! HE USED HIS WITCH BLOOD TO SAVE THE BOY! HE SAVED HIM WITH DARK MAGIC!
SAVE ME!
PLEASE!

I'M SORRY. I'LL DO WHAT I CAN, BUT THERE'S ONLY SO MUCH OF ME TO GO AROUND.
WHAT THE HELL'S GOING ON IN HERE? ARE YOU INSANE? WHY AREN'T YOU SUITED UP?
GET HIM! OPEN HIM UP AND GET HIS MAGIC BLOOD!
OOF!

HEY!
I'M SORRY. I'M SO DAMN SORRY.

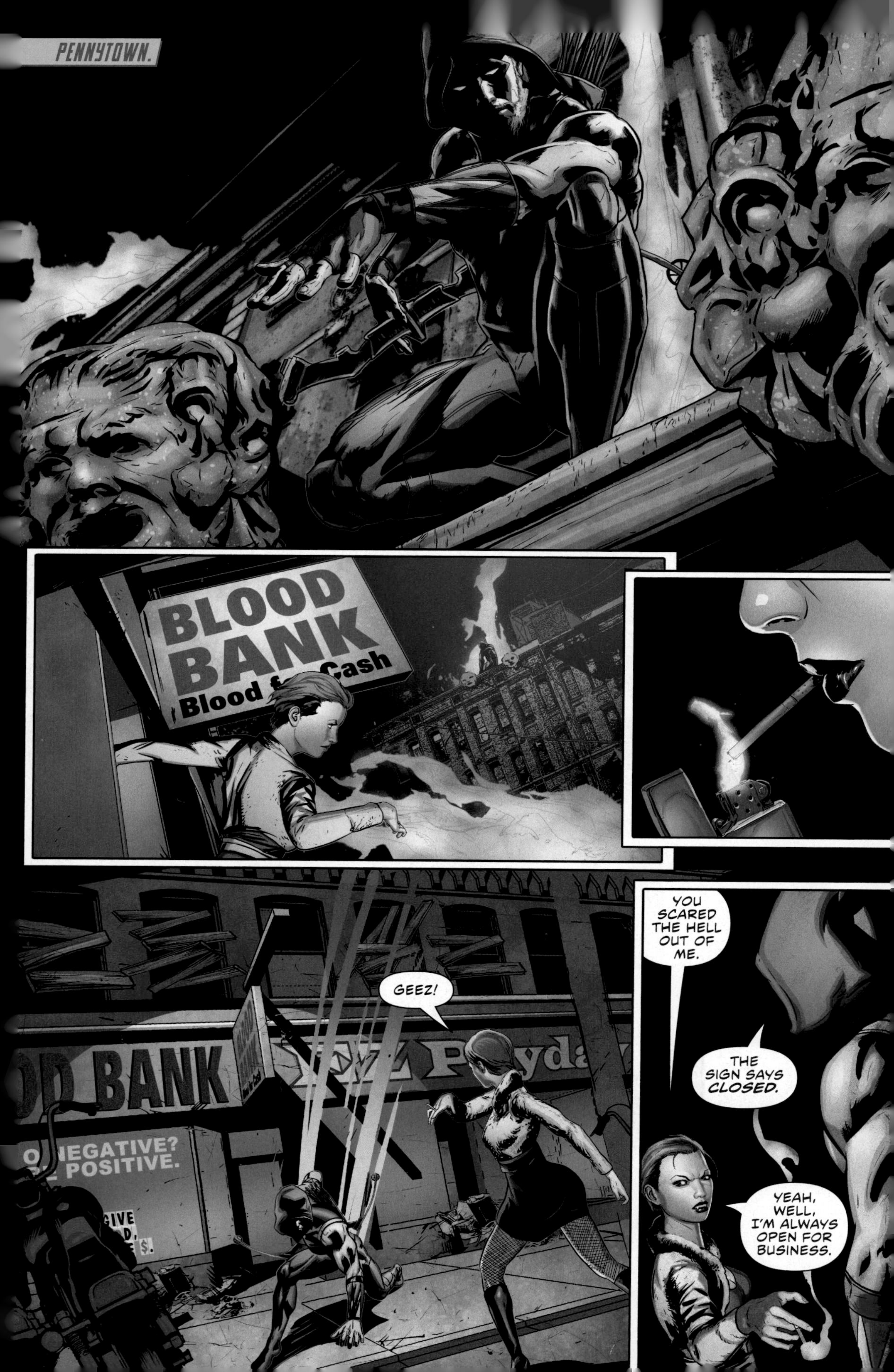
PENNYTOWN.
BLOOD BANK
Blood f... Cash
GEEZ!
...OD BANK
O NEGATIVE?
...E POSITIVE.
YOU SCARED THE HELL OUT OF ME.
THE SIGN SAYS CLOSED.
YEAH, WELL, I'M ALWAYS OPEN FOR BUSINESS.

WHAT'S GOING ON IN THERE?
I NEED TO KNOW. IT'S THE BERSERKERS, ISN'T IT?
INSTEAD OF BITING, THEY'RE BLEEDING, QUIETLY BUILDING AN ARMY.
AND THEN I SMELL IT. HER BREATH, LIKE MINE, IS AS BITTERLY ODORED AS PENNIES.
GET AWAY FROM ME!
YOU'RE INFECTED...
...YOU NEED TO GET REGISTERED, MEDICATED. YOU NEED HELP.
FOLLOW YOUR OWN ADVICE, *HERO*.
I COULD SMELL THE DOG ON YOU FROM FIFTY YARDS AWAY.

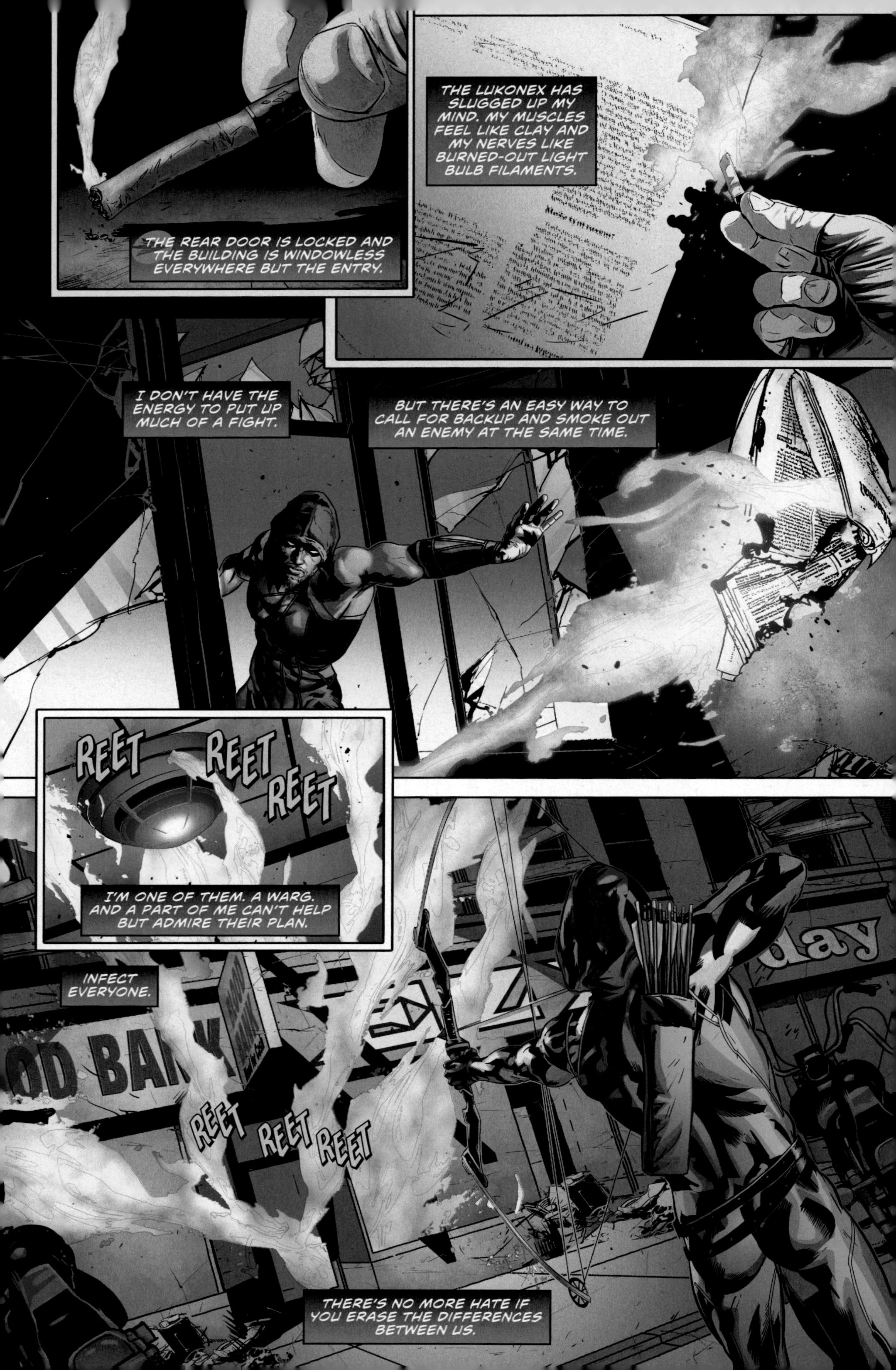
THE REAR DOOR IS LOCKED AND THE BUILDING IS WINDOWLESS EVERYWHERE BUT THE ENTRY.
THE LUKONEX HAS SLUGGED UP MY MIND. MY MUSCLES FEEL LIKE CLAY AND MY NERVES LIKE BURNED-OUT LIGHT BULB FILAMENTS.
I DON'T HAVE THE ENERGY TO PUT UP MUCH OF A FIGHT.
BUT THERE'S AN EASY WAY TO CALL FOR BACKUP AND SMOKE OUT AN ENEMY AT THE SAME TIME.
REET REET REET
I'M ONE OF THEM. A WARG. AND A PART OF ME CAN'T HELP BUT ADMIRE THEIR PLAN.
INFECT EVERYONE.
OD BAN
day
REET REET REET
THERE'S NO MORE HATE IF YOU ERASE THE DIFFERENCES BETWEEN US.

...OH NO.
HELL, NO.
REET
REET
REET
REET
REET
Hmmm.
REET REET
REET
REET
REET

TING
TING
TING
REET REET
REET
KNOCK, KNOCK. ANYBODY HOME?
WE HEARD THERE MIGHT BE SOME NAUGHTY PUPPIES HOLED UP IN HERE.
NOT BITING? THEN MAYBE THIS WILL GET YOUR ATTENTION.

CRASH
CRASH
CLANG
COME ON, GUYS. LET'S MARK OUR TERRITORY.
ZZZZZIP
THROUGHOUT OUR HISTORY, YOU STAB US, LYNCH US, SHOOT US, CRIMINALIZE US. DISRESPECT US.
Huh?

ALL MY PEOPLE WANT IS TO BE TREATED LIKE EVERYONE ELSE.
YOU'RE NOT PEOPLE! YOU'RE A DISEASE!
BLAT
BLAT

WHAT CAN I DO? FIRE A BROADHEAD INTO AN EYE? STUN THEM WITH A DETONATION?
I DON'T ALIGN WITH EITHER SIDE, AND I'M TOO WEAK TO FIGHT THEM ALL.
MAYBE I SHOULD JUST LET THEM DESTROY THEMSELVES.
MAYBE THAT WOULD BE FOR THE BEST.
YOU'RE THE ONE WHO SHOTGUNNED MY HAND AT THE MIDNIGHT PARADE.
FOR THAT ALONE, I SHOULD TEAR OUT YOUR THROAT.

BUT TO EVEN THE SCORE, I'VE GOT AN EVEN BETTER IDEA.
BLESS
NOW YOU ARE WHAT YOU HATE, MY FELLOW WARG.
NOOOOO!
JIMMY! JIMMY, GET OVER HERE!
WHAT'S WRONG, ANDREW? ARE YOU SHOT?
PUD-A-PUD-A-PUD-A
CUT IT OFF! CUT IT OFF BEFORE IT'S TOO LATE!
RUM-RUM-RUUUM
YAAAAAARGH!
RUM-RUM-RUUUMM

I HADN'T MADE UP MY MIND WHAT TO DO. TURNS OUT, I DIDN'T HAVE TO.
A BRIGADE OF COP CARS AND FIRE TRUCKS SHOWED UP AND EVERYONE SCATTERED.
SO-- WAIT--LET E GET THIS STRAIGHT.
JUST LET M RIP EACH APART? THAT T SOUND LIKE U, OLLIE.
IN THE NEWS, WHENEVER SOMEBODY TACKLES A CRAZED GUNMA OR RUNS INTO A BURNING BUILDING TO SAVE A BABY YOU KNOW WHAT THEY SAY?
"I DIDN'T THINK ABOUT IT." "IT WAS GUT INSTINCT."
BEING A HERO IS INBORN, AUTOMATIC.
NOT DELIBERATELY REASONED.
THIS WHOLE THING--GREEN ARROW-- IT'S ME ACTING INTENTIONALLY, TRYING SO HARD TO DO GOOD, RECTIFYING THE DISGUSTINGLY SELFISH PERSON I USED TO BE.
IT'S NOT INSTINCTIVE. IT'S A PERFORMANCE, WITH ME MULLING OVER EVERY MOVE.

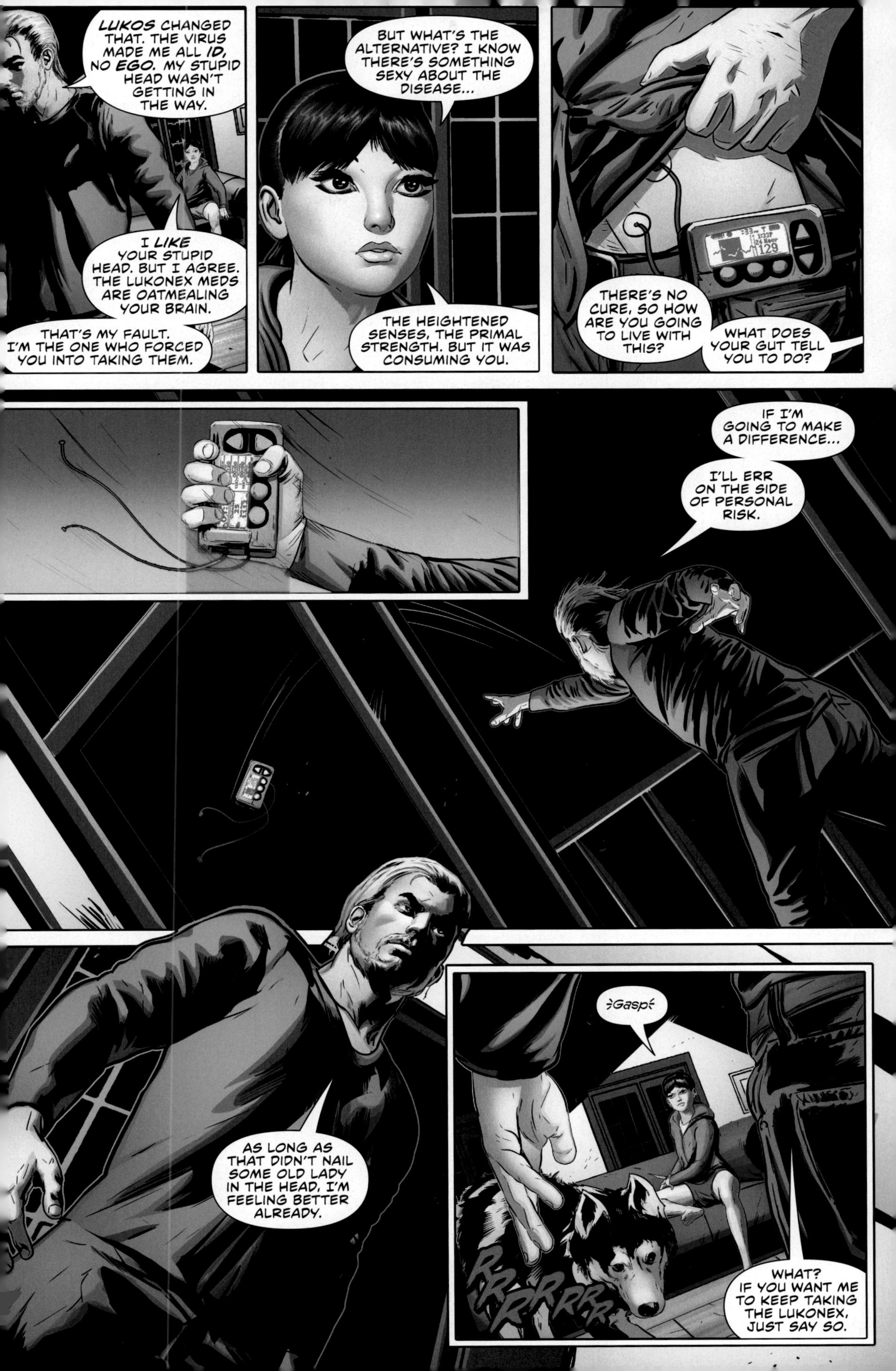
LUKOS CHANGED THAT. THE VIRUS MADE ME ALL ID, NO EGO. MY STUPID HEAD WASN'T GETTING IN THE WAY.
I LIKE YOUR STUPID HEAD. BUT I AGREE. THE LUKONEX MEDS ARE OATMEALING YOUR BRAIN.
THAT'S MY FAULT. I'M THE ONE WHO FORCED YOU INTO TAKING THEM.
BUT WHAT'S THE ALTERNATIVE? I KNOW THERE'S SOMETHING SEXY ABOUT THE DISEASE...
THE HEIGHTENED SENSES, THE PRIMAL STRENGTH. BUT IT WAS CONSUMING YOU.
129
THERE'S NO CURE, SO HOW ARE YOU GOING TO LIVE WITH THIS?
WHAT DOES YOUR GUT TELL YOU TO DO?
IF I'M GOING TO MAKE A DIFFERENCE...
I'LL ERR ON THE SIDE OF PERSONAL RISK.
AS LONG AS THAT DIDN'T NAIL SOME OLD LADY IN THE HEAD, I'M FEELING BETTER ALREADY.
Gasp
RRRRRRRR
WHAT? IF YOU WANT ME TO KEEP TAKING THE LUKONEX, JUST SAY SO.

DESTROY, DESTROY, DESTROY!
IT'S OKAY. I SHOULD HAVE TOLD YOU. HENRY REFABBED ONE OF ZIMM'S DRONES.
DO YOU NEED A MINUTE, EMI? TO GO CHANGE YOUR UNDERWEAR, I MEAN.
HENRY, I'M GOING TO INTRODUCE YOU TO INTRICATE NETWORKS OF PAIN YOU DIDN'T KNOW EXISTED.
WHAT ARE YOU DOING HERE, HENRY?
I KNOW YOU FOUND THE SOURCE OF INFECTION AT THE BLOOD CENTERS, BUT THE PARAGON MANSION WASN'T A BUST.
WE MAY HAVE FOUND A WAY TO END THIS.

PARAGON MANSION BEDROOM.
YOUR GUEST HAS ARRIVED, SIR.
THE WORLD'S GREATEST MERCENARY? THE WORLD'S GREATEST ASSASSIN?
MORE LIKE THE WORLD'S GREEDIEST, MOST INCOMPETENT ONE-EYED LEECH.
...HOW MUCH MONEY HAVE I PAID YOU ALREADY? AND YOU STILL HAVEN'T FOUND HIM?
THUNK

I SUGGEST YOU CHANGE YOUR TONE, OLD MAN.
OR I'LL OPEN YOU UP AND WHITTLE YOU DOWN TO THE MARROW.

WHAT NEWS DO YOU BRING?
THE PROMISING KIND.
THE MIRACLE WORKER? THE BLOOD CURE?
I'VE FOUND HIM. I'M CERTAIN OF IT. HE WAS FIRST IN LIBERIA. PART OF AN EBOLA QUARANTINE UNIT.
AND NOW?
MY SOURCES SAY NIGERIA. WHEREVER PEOPLE ARE DYING, HE GOES.
THEN WHAT ARE YOU WAITING FOR? THERE'S NOT A MINUTE TO LOSE. *GO!*
STOP!
YOU KNOW, I REALLY DON'T CARE WHAT MY CLIENTS WANT. I ONLY CARE THAT THEY PAY ME.
BUT IN THIS CASE, I CAN'T HELP BUT FEEL LIKE YOU NEED A GENTLE REMINDER:
YOU'VE CLEARLY EXCEEDED YOUR EXPIRATION DATE.
THAT BLOOD IS THE ONLY THING KEEPING ME ALIVE!
HOW BADLY DO YOU WANT THIS MAN?
MORE THAN ANYTHING! HE'S A LIVING INOCULATION.
HIS BLOOD CAN CURE ANY DISEASE AND INFIRMITY. IT WILL SAVE ME, PRESERVE ME, REGENERATE ME.

I DELIVER THIS SO-CALLED MIRACLE TO YOU WITHIN A WEEK AND YOU ADD ANOTHER FIVE MILLION TO THE PURSE.
AND IF YOU FAIL TO DO SO?
THEN I HAVE A PROPOSAL.
I FORFEIT MY FEE ENTIRELY.
DID YOU HEAR THAT, DANA? IN ONE WEEK, I'LL RISE FROM THIS BED!
I'LL DANCE THE FOXTROT!
I'LL CLIMB MOUNT RAINIER. I'LL MAKE LOVE TO THREE WOMEN--NO, FIVE!--AT THE SAME TIME.
IF WHAT YOU SAY ABOUT THIS MAN IS TRUE, HE COULD SAVE THOUSANDS, MAYBE MILLIONS OF LIVES...
WHOSE LIVES? AFRICANS? WHAT DIFFERENCE WOULD IT MAKE? IT'S A LOST CONTINENT.
YOU DON'T KNOW A DAMN THING, OLD MAN. AFRICA IS THE WOMB OF THE WORLD.
HERE'S WHAT I KNOW: YOU DON'T AMASS A FORTUNE BY WRINGING YOUR HANDS OVER OTHER PEOPLE'S TROUBLES.
SURELY A MAN LIKE YOU CAN UNDERSTAND THAT.

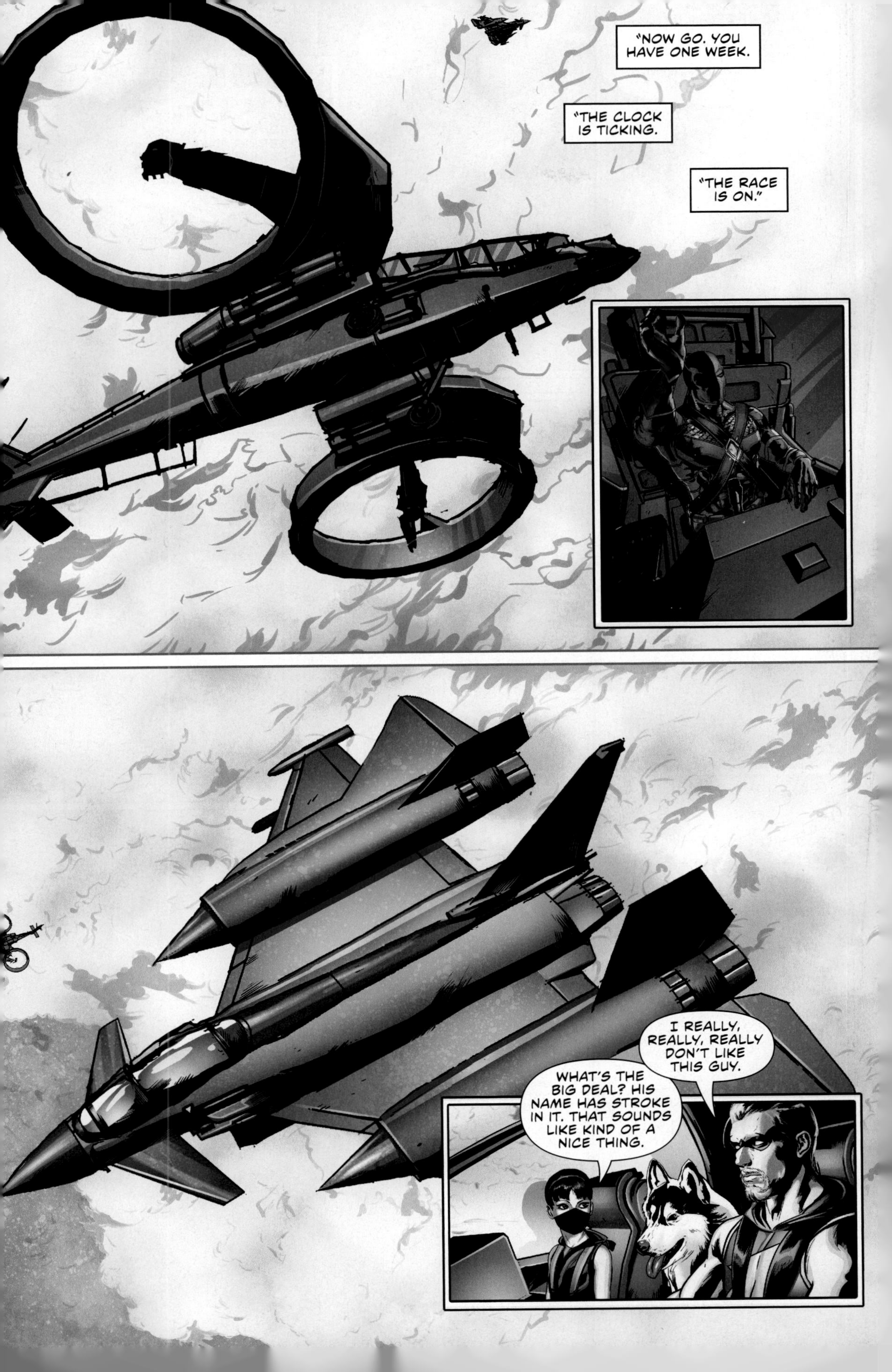
"NOW GO. YOU HAVE ONE WEEK.
"THE CLOCK IS TICKING.
"THE RACE IS ON."
I REALLY, REALLY, REALLY DON'T LIKE THIS GUY.
WHAT'S THE BIG DEAL? HIS NAME HAS STROKE IN IT. THAT SOUNDS LIKE KIND OF A NICE THING.

HAVE YOU EVER FELT OVERWHELMED BY THE NUMBER OF STARS IN THE SKY? OR BEWILDERINGLY CONSIDERED THE NUMBER OF GRAINS OF SAND THAT MIGHT ADD UP TO A BEACH?
THIS GUY'S KILL LIST IS A LITTLE LIKE THAT.
BET I COULD TAKE HIM.
THAT'S THE ATTITUDE OF A FUTURE CORPSE.
WE'RE ALL WEAKER THAN WE SEEM. UNDERNEATH THE MASK, THERE'S ALWAYS A MESSED-UP, VULNERABLE HUMAN.
HE'S PROBABLY CRIES HIMSELF TO SLEEP CLUTCHING A TEDDY BEAR.
NOT DEATHSTROKE. THEY CALL HIM TERMINATOR FOR A REASON.
HE'S SO BIG AND SCARY, JUST BLOW HIM OUT OF THE SKY!
"THIS JET IS OUTFITTED WITH A CLOAKING TECHNOLOGY IN DEVELOPMENT AT QUEEN INDUSTRIES.
"IT USES HEXAGONAL CONFIGURATIO OF GLASS-LIK PANELS TO BEN LIGHT, MAKING IT DIFFICULT T SEE AND CATC ON RADAR.
"OUR STRATEGY IS INVISIBILITY. AND WILL REMAIN SO.
"WE'RE HEADED INTO A WAR ZONE.

"THIS SO-CALLED HEALER--
ITH HIS MIRACLE BLOOD--HE
IGHT BE MY ONLY CHANCE,
SEATTLE'S ONLY CHANCE.
"DEATHSTROKE KNOWS
WHERE TO FIND HIM.
WE DON'T.
"FOR NOW
WE FOLLOW
HIS LEAD.
"HE ONLY
HAS ONE EYE.
"LET'S HOPE HE
KEEPS IT TRAINED ON
THE WAY AHEAD.
"AND NOT
BEHIND."

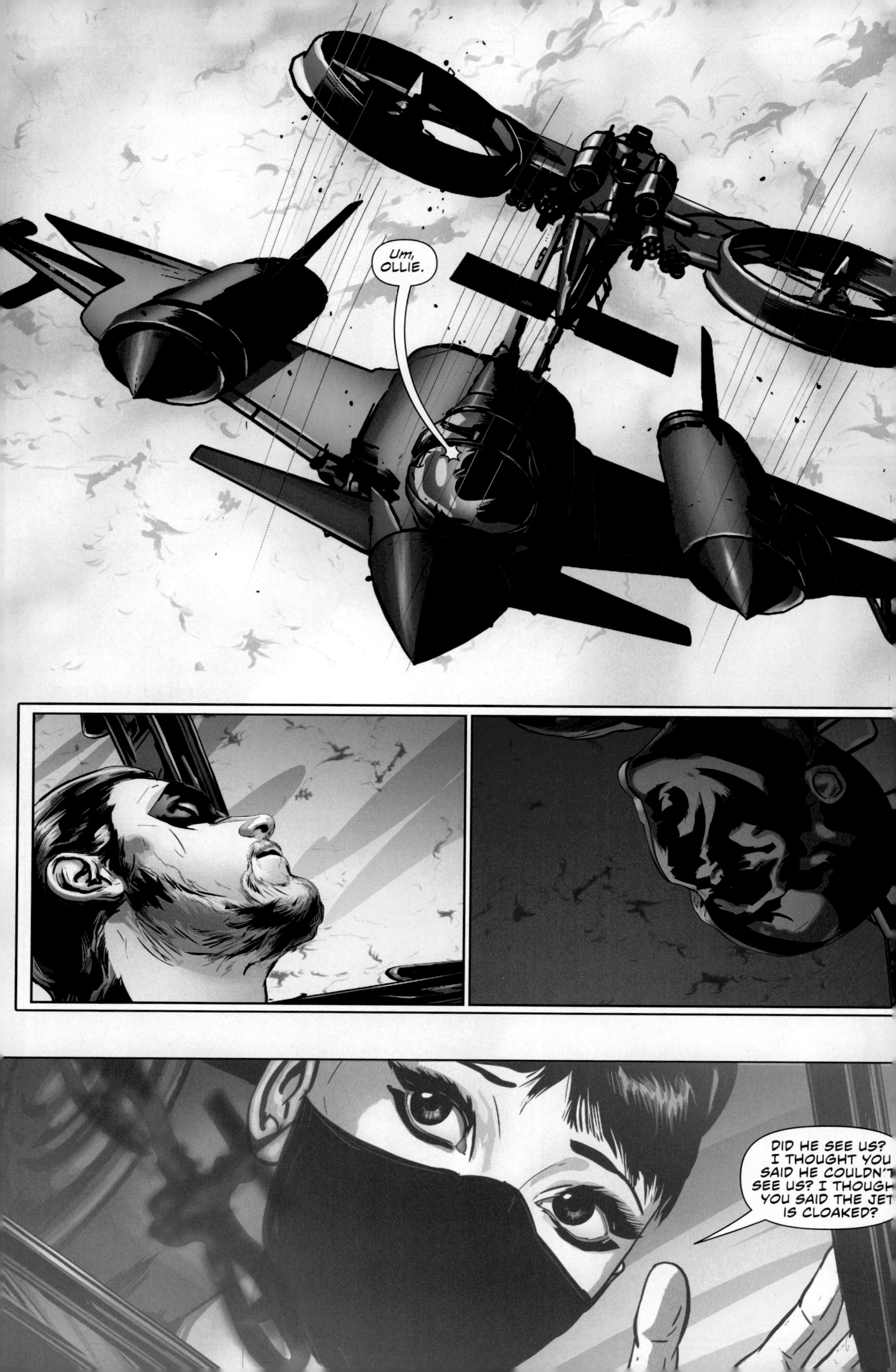
Um, OLLIE.
DID HE SEE US? I THOUGHT YOU SAID HE COULDN'T SEE US? I THOUGH YOU SAID THE JET IS CLOAKED?

YOU.
WHAT ARE YOU DOING HERE? AND WHY ARE YOU EVEN ALIVE?
HAVEN'T I GOTTEN AROUND TO KILLING YOU YET?
IT'S DIFFICULT TO KEEP TRACK SOMETIMES.
KA-TOOM
I SAID THE CLOAKING TECHNOLOGY WAS IN DEVELOPMENT.
WE'RE STILL HAVING BETA PROBLEMS.

DEET DEET DEET
GEORGE! COME HERE, BOY! IN MY LAP!
OUT OF THE FRYING PAN, INTO THE FIRE!

KA-BOOM

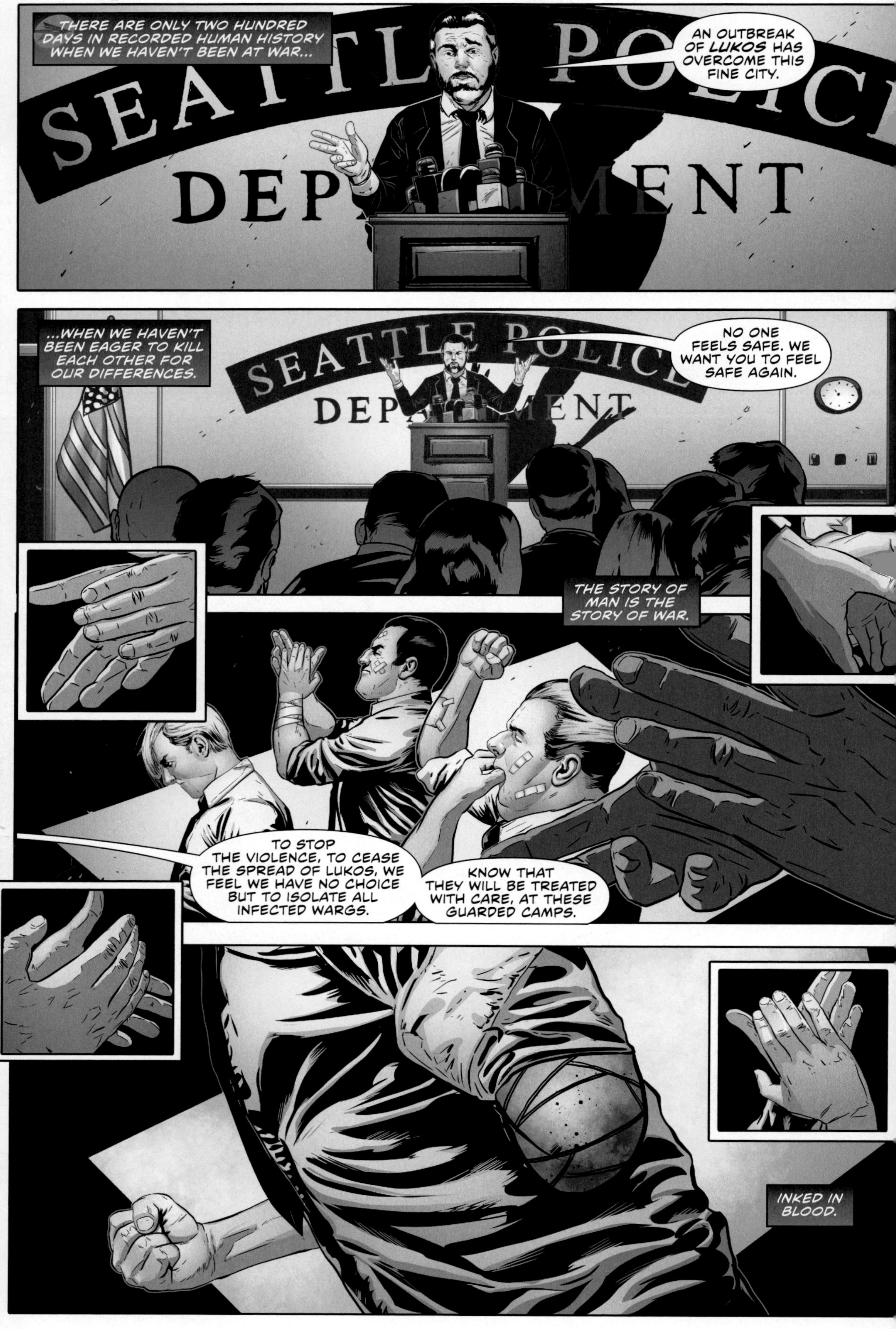
THERE ARE ONLY TWO HUNDRED DAYS IN RECORDED HUMAN HISTORY WHEN WE HAVEN'T BEEN AT WAR...
SEATTLE POLICE DEPARTMENT
AN OUTBREAK OF LUKOS HAS OVERCOME THIS FINE CITY.
...WHEN WE HAVEN'T BEEN EAGER TO KILL EACH OTHER FOR OUR DIFFERENCES.
NO ONE FEELS SAFE. WE WANT YOU TO FEEL SAFE AGAIN.
THE STORY OF MAN IS THE STORY OF WAR.
TO STOP THE VIOLENCE, TO CEASE THE SPREAD OF LUKOS, WE FEEL WE HAVE NO CHOICE BUT TO ISOLATE ALL INFECTED WARGS.
KNOW THAT THEY WILL BE TREATED WITH CARE, AT THESE GUARDED CAMPS.
INKED IN BLOOD.

MY CITY IS AT WAR.
MY BODY IS AT WAR.
MY WORLD IS AT WAR.
VROOOOM

HOW COULD I EVER HOPE TO FIND A CURE?
IT WOULD TAKE A MIRACLE...

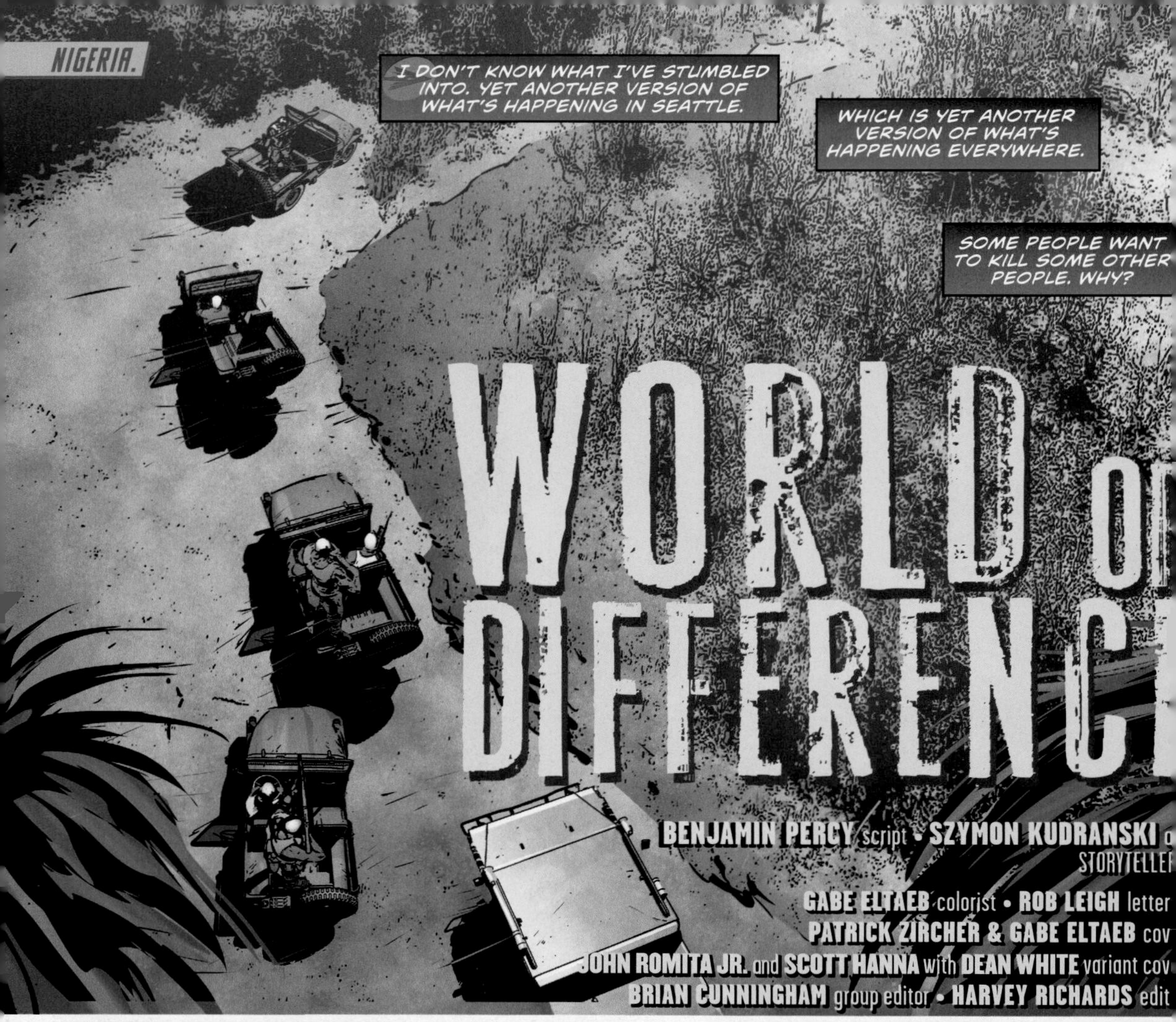
NIGERIA.
I DON'T KNOW WHAT I'VE STUMBLED INTO. YET ANOTHER VERSION OF WHAT'S HAPPENING IN SEATTLE.
WHICH IS YET ANOTHER VERSION OF WHAT'S HAPPENING EVERYWHERE.
SOME PEOPLE WANT TO KILL SOME OTHER PEOPLE. WHY?
WORLD OF DIFFERENC
BENJAMIN PERCY script • SZYMON KUDRANSKI a
STORYTELLEI
GABE ELTAEB colorist • ROB LEIGH letter
PATRICK ZIRCHER & GABE ELTAEB cov
JOHN ROMITA JR. and SCOTT HANNA with DEAN WHITE variant cov
BRIAN CUNNINGHAM group editor • HARVEY RICHARDS edit

DIFFERENCES. REGIONAL, RELIGIOUS, ETHNIC, POLITICAL DIFFERENCES.
THAT'S OUR UNIVERSAL DISEASE, AS HUMANS. DIFFERENCE REPELS US.

I'M HERE TO HUNT DOWN A HEALER, A MAN WITH MIRACLE BLOOD...
...A DOSE OF WHICH MIGHT CURE THE LUKOS VIRUS RAVAGING MY BODY AND BRING PEACE TO THE STREETS OF SEATTLE.

BUT MAYBE THIS IS A HOPELESS QUEST.
YOU CAN'T CURE HATE, AFTER ALL.
WELCOME, WELCOME! I'M SO DELIGHTED YOU'RE HERE.
WHO ARE YOU PEOPLE?
MY NAME IS OGA AND WE ARE THE WHITES.
THE WHITES?
FOR CENTURIES YOU HAVE STOLEN EVERYTHING FROM US--OUR LAND, OUR BODIES, OUR DIAMONDS AND GOLD, OUR COFFEE, EVEN OUR CHOCOLATE.
IN RESPONSE I ATE UP ALL YOUR STRATEGIES, YOUR IMPERIALIST PRIVILEGE--STUDYING AT OXFORD, AT PRINCETON--AND BROUGHT THEM HOME AS MY WEAPON.
CALL IT AN EXERCISE IN CULTURAL APPROPRIATION.
SO YES, WE ARE THE WHITES. WE ARE THE PILLAGERS, THE BLOOD-STARVED NEO-COLONIALISTS.
AND YOU KNOW WHAT? WE'RE WINNING. YOUR WAY WORKS.

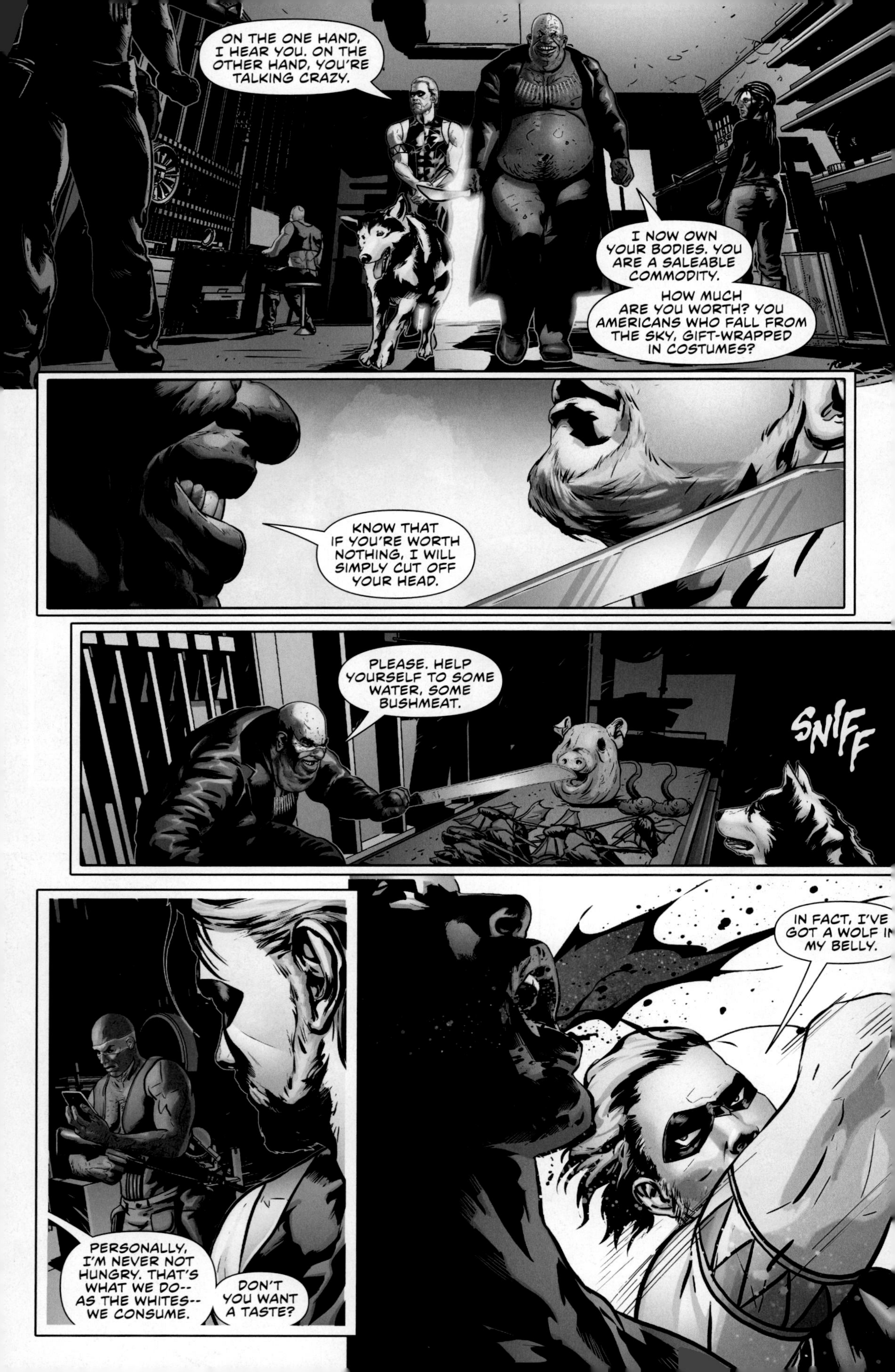
ON THE ONE HAND, I HEAR YOU. ON THE OTHER HAND, YOU'RE TALKING CRAZY.
I NOW OWN YOUR BODIES. YOU ARE A SALEABLE COMMODITY.
HOW MUCH ARE YOU WORTH? YOU AMERICANS WHO FALL FROM THE SKY, GIFT-WRAPPED IN COSTUMES?
KNOW THAT IF YOU'RE WORTH NOTHING, I WILL SIMPLY CUT OFF YOUR HEAD.
PLEASE. HELP YOURSELF TO SOME WATER, SOME BUSHMEAT.
SNIFF
PERSONALLY, I'M NEVER NOT HUNGRY. THAT'S WHAT WE DO-- AS THE WHITES-- WE CONSUME.
DON'T YOU WANT A TASTE?
IN FACT, I'VE GOT A WOLF IN MY BELLY.

CRUNCH
NOW WOULD BE A GOOD TIME TO STOP, MY FRIENDS.
YAAAAAAA!
I REALLY WOULD PREFER NOT TO KILL YOU.
THE DEAD AREN'T WORTH MORE THAN THE COINS LAID OVER THEIR EYES.

IT HURTS, OGA! IT'S BROKEN!
SOMEONE FETCH THE DOCTOR!
THERE IS SOMETHING WRONG WITH YOU, MY FRIEND?
OR SHOULD I SAY, THERE IS SOMETHING SPECIAL ABOUT YOU?
I'M A WARG. SEEMS LIKE I CHANGE MY MIND DAILY AS TO WHETHER THE INFECTION DOOMS OR BLESSES ME.
A BLESSING, I'D SAY. YOU'VE GOT CLAWS INSIDE OF YOU. I DO TOO. AND FANGS AND FUR AND TAILS AND HOOVES.
I FEEL AS THOUGH I'VE DRANK WHOLE RIVERS AND EATEN WHOLE VILLAGES. AND YET I STILL WANT MORE.
DO YOU EVER FEEL THAT WAY? THE MORE IS IN YOU, THE GREATER YOUR CAPACITY FOR HUNGER?
MUNCH MUNCH

HERE IS THE DOCTOR, OGA.
I'D LIKE YOU TO MEET ANOTHER GUEST OF MINE. HE'S WORTH FAR MORE THAN YOU ARE. AN UNFATHOMABLE AMOUNT REALLY.
COME ON, DOCTOR. YOU'VE GOT A PATIENT WHO NEEDS YOU.
SAY, "AH."
PLEASE, PLEASE. IT HURTS.
NOT FOR LONG.
IT'S WORKING! I CAN FEEL THE HOLY LIGHT IN MY VEINS.

I FEEL VERY AMERICAN WHEN I SAY THIS...
...BUT WITH SO MANY BLESSINGS, IT'S IMPOSSIBLE NOT TO BELIEVE THAT GOD IS ON OUR SIDE.
IT'S A MIRACLE!
I COULD SHOOT THE TAIL OFF A GIRAFFE AT FIFTY YARDS.
YOU TALK BIG, BIG MAN. FINISH THAT BOTTLE. THE WE DO SOME TARG PRACTICE.
BLAMBLAM
BLA
BLAM
BLAM
HA HA HA!
THE SUN WAS IN MY EYE! YOU'RE SUC A SNIPER, YOU SHOW ME HOW IT'S DONE.
WATCH HOW THE REAL ASSASSIN DOES IT.
BLAM
SCR

FINE. YOU WIN.
BUT... I NEVER PULLED THE TRIGGER.
THEN WHO?
I'M THE GUY WHO CAN SHOOT THE TAIL OFF A GIRAFFE AT FIFTY YARDS. WHO ARE YOU?

WE FOUND THE GOOD DOCTOR IN A TRENCH WE HAD DUG. A TRENCH FOR THE DEAD.
THEY WEREN'T ALL DEAD. NOT YET.
AND HE WAS BRINGING THEM BACK TO LIFE.
I CAN ONLY HEAL THE LIVING.
THAT'S OUR GUY. DOCTOR MIRACLE.
LET'S JUST TAKE HIM BY TH HAND AND SKIP HAPPILY OUT OF HERE.
"AFRICA IS MANY THINGS. FIFTY COUNTRIES, ONE THOUSAND LANGUAGES, NEARLY A BILLION PEOPLE.
"BUT IF I CAN'T BE KILLED, IF THE WHITES CAN'T BE KILLED, AFRICA BECOMES ONE THING: OURS.
"WE'LL SWALLOW IT WHOLE."
KA-BOOM
BLAT BLAT
BLAT BLAT

WHO WOULD DARE ATTACK US?
NOW YOU REALLY SOUND LIKE AN AMERICAN.
YOU KNOW WHO IT IS, DON'T YOU? WHO IS IT, WOLF MAN?
I'VE GOT A GUESS.
"AND FOR BOTH OUR SAKES, I HOPE I'M WRONG."
BLAT
DOOM
DOOM
BLAT
BLAT
BLAT

"I NARROWLY MISSED YOU IN NORTH KOREA.
BLAT BLAT BLAT BLAT
SSSSSSST
"I FOUND EVIDENCE OF YOU IN INDIA, IN UKRAINE, ALL OVER SYR
BOOM
"WHEREVER THE WAS DEATH, THE WERE RUMORS O YOU. WE HAVE TH IN COMMON.
I SHOULD HAVE GUESSED I WOULD FIND YOU HERE, DOCTOR MIRACLE.
IN AFRICA.
A CONTINENT CONSTANTLY EMBATTLED...
...BECAUSE WHO WOULDN'T BE WILLING TO FIGHT FOR THE SOURCE OF ALL LIFE?

HE'S SLAUGHTERING US!
KARMA IS A BITCH.
HSTROKE LIVED IN AFRICA FOR OME TIME. I'M GUESSING HE SN'T LIKE WHAT YOU'VE DONE TO THE PLACE.
HAT ES HE ANT?
THE SAME THING WE'RE HERE FOR. THIS MAN. DOCTOR MIRACLE.
WHY IS THE WORLD ALWAYS BLEEDING? WHY MUST I BE THE BANDAGE?
DON'T TAKE YOUR EYES OFF THEM OR YOUR FINGERS OFF THE TRIGGER!
I'LL
huff huff
I'LL MAKE BUSHMEAT OUT OF HIM.

huff huff
THUT THUT THUT THUT THUT
THUT THUT
THUT THUT
THUT
THUT THUT
THUT THUT THUT THUT THUT
THUT THUT THUT
THUT THUT THUT
THUT THUT

THUT THUT THUT THUT
THUT THUT THUT THUT THUT
THUT THUT THUT THUT THUT THUT THUT THUT THUT THUT THUT THUT THUT THUT
YOU ARE NOT DEATH. I AM DEATH! I AM...
THUT THUT THUT THUT THUT THUT THU
...DEATH.

THUD

UNSOLICITED ADVICE.
RUN.
THIS IS THE END OF THE SAFARI.
I CAN EITHER HURL A GRENADE INSIDE.
OR YOU COULD SIMPLY COME OUT.

YOU'RE FASTER THAN I REMEMBER.
YELP
STRONGER, TOO.

AND QUITE
BIT UGLIER,
MUST SAY.
SNICK

YOU MIGHT BE A WOLF...
...BUT I REMAIN THE ALPHA.

I'VE TRAVELED MANY THOUSANDS OF MILES AND SPILLED MANY HUNDREDS OF GALLONS OF BLOOD, LOOKING FOR YOU.
PLEASE. I DON'T WANT TO BE ANYONE'S WEAPON.

"I WANT TO HELP.
"NOT HURT."
NO, OLLIE. NO, NO, NO.
YOU'RE NOT ALLOWED TO DIE.

GABE
ELTAEB

ERIA.
SOME BELIEVE YOU CAN READ BLOOD THE SAME WAY YOU CAN READ A PALM OR AN ASTROLOGICAL CALENDAR...
...PREDICTING YOUR PERSONALITY, YOUR JOB, YOUR LOVE...
...YOUR DEATH.
I'M AB+, THE MOST SELFISH BLOOD TYPE, ABLE TO ACCEPT ANY DONOR BUT GIVE ONLY TO OTHERS LIKE ME.
FOR A LONG TIME THAT WAS THE HOROSCOPE I DESERVED.
GET AWAY FROM HIM!
RANSFUSION
BENJAMIN PERCY script
SZYMON KUDRANSKI art
GABE ELTAEB colorist
DAVE SHARPE letterer
SZYMON KUDRANSKI cover
SZYMON KUDRANSKI homage variant cover
BRIAN CUNNINGHAM group editor
HARVEY RICHARDS editor

BUT PEOPLE CHANGE.
I CHANGED.
I'M CHANGING, EVEN NOW.
THE MACHETE WAS STILL WET WITH DOCTOR MIRACLE'S BLOOD.
HEALING THE VERY WOUND IT RENDERED WHILE CLEANSING ME OF THE LUKOS VIRUS.
WHEN DEATHSTROKE STABBED ME, HE SAVED M

LUKOS MADE ME FEEL MORE THAN HUMAN, IMPROVED, SUPER.
GASP!
A BIO-CHEMICAL CHEAT FOR MY INBORN DEFICIENCY IN CHARACTER.
BUT I'VE LEARNED GREATNESS ISN'T ASSIGNED OR DIAGNOSED.
IT'S EARNED.
OLLIE?
OLLIE!
YOU'RE BETTER.
BETTER? I FEEL LIKE AN OLD MAN THAT'S BROKEN THROUGH THE SEAMS OF A YOUNG MAN COSTUME.
BUT I'M ALIVE. I MADE IT THROUGH THE THRESHER.

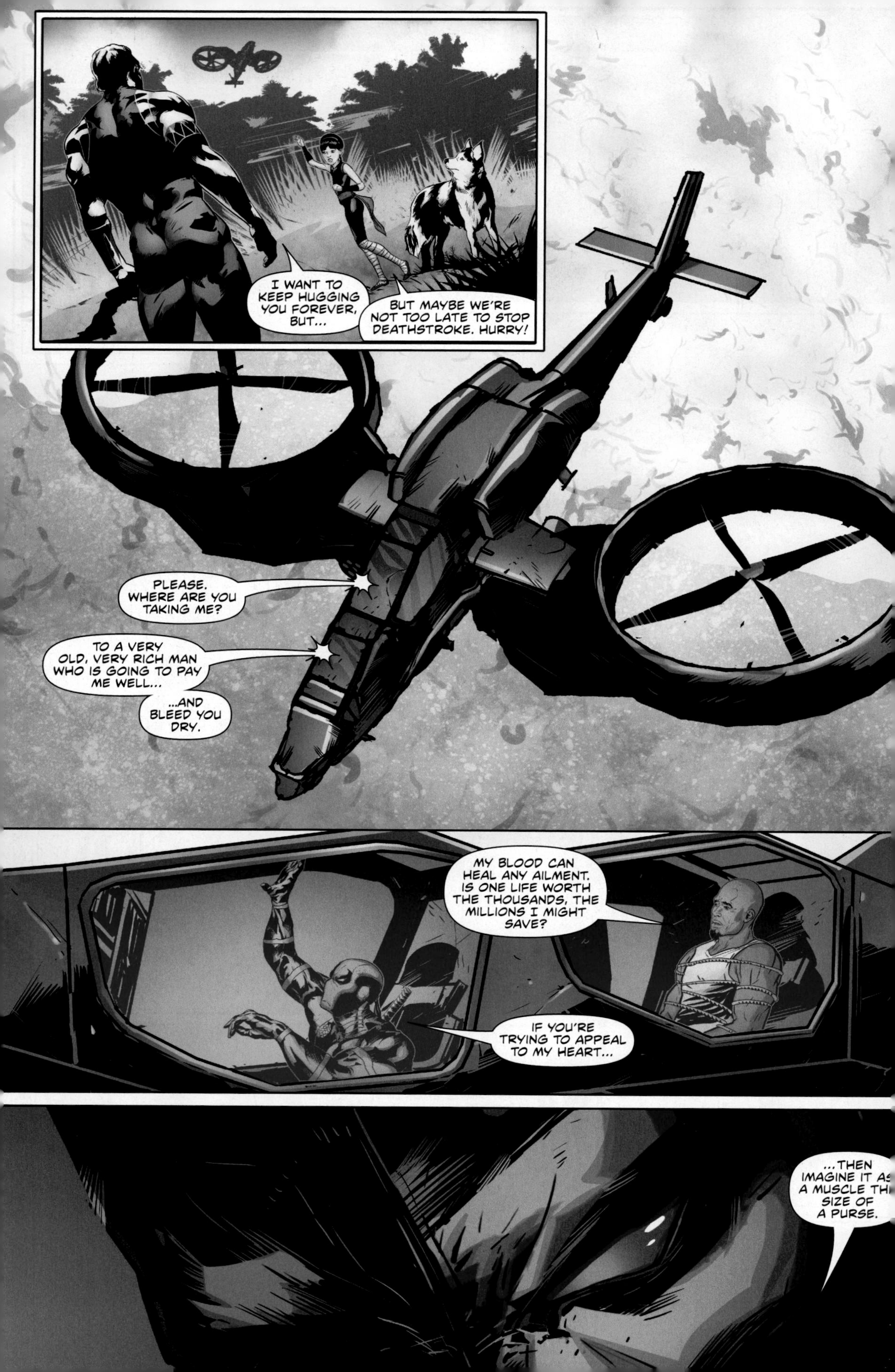
I WANT TO KEEP HUGGING YOU FOREVER, BUT...
BUT MAYBE WE'RE NOT TOO LATE TO STOP DEATHSTROKE. HURRY!
PLEASE. WHERE ARE YOU TAKING ME?
TO A VERY OLD, VERY RICH MAN WHO IS GOING TO PAY ME WELL...
...AND BLEED YOU DRY.
MY BLOOD CAN HEAL ANY AILMENT. IS ONE LIFE WORTH THE THOUSANDS, THE MILLIONS I MIGHT SAVE?
IF YOU'RE TRYING TO APPEAL TO MY HEART...
...THEN IMAGINE IT AS A MUSCLE THE SIZE OF A PURSE.

"WHAT ARE WE SUPPOSED TO DO NOW?" SHE SAID, HOPELESSLY.
WISH I KNEW.
I'M OUT OF WISHES, OLLIE. I USED THEM ALL UP ON YOU.
WOOF!
OR...WE COULD WALK? SWIM? PADDLEBOARD? ROLLERBLADE?
ANYTHING BUT FLY THAT THING.
YOU SEE WHAT DOCTOR MIRACLE DID FOR ME? IMAGINE WHAT HE COULD DO FOR SEATTLE.
THE CITY NEEDS TO BE INOCULATED BEFORE IT RIPS ITSELF APART.
I HEAR YOU. I'M JUST NOT SURE THAT DO-WHAT-THE-DOG-SAYS IS A GREAT STRATEGY.

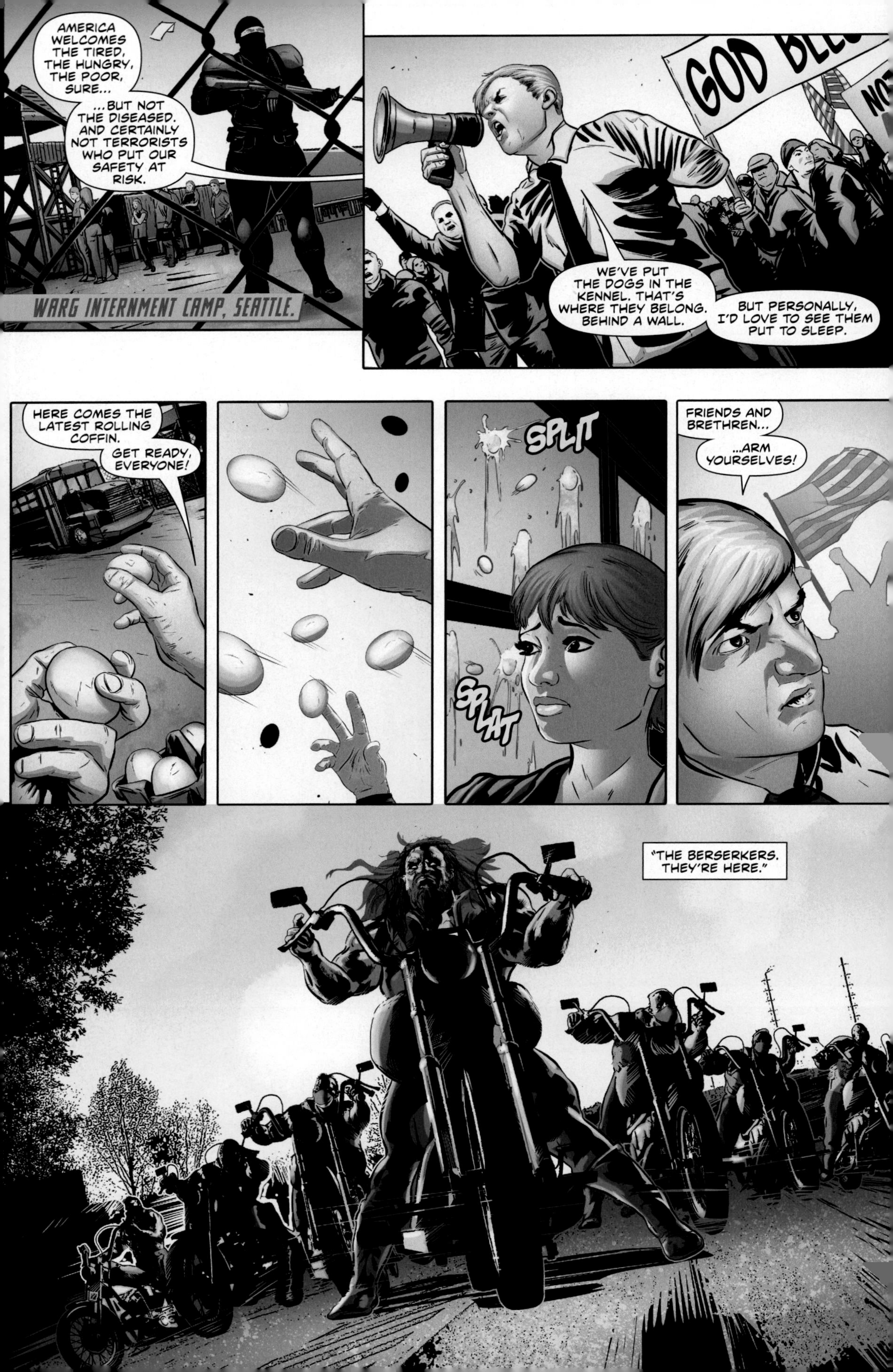
AMERICA WELCOMES THE TIRED, THE HUNGRY, THE POOR, SURE...
...BUT NOT THE DISEASED. AND CERTAINLY NOT TERRORISTS WHO PUT OUR SAFETY AT RISK.
WARG INTERNMENT CAMP, SEATTLE.
GOD BLE
NO
WE'VE PUT THE DOGS IN THE KENNEL. THAT'S WHERE THEY BELONG. BEHIND A WALL.
BUT PERSONALLY, I'D LOVE TO SEE THEM PUT TO SLEEP.
HERE COMES THE LATEST ROLLING COFFIN.
GET READY, EVERYONE!
SPLIT
SPLAT
FRIENDS AND BRETHREN...
...ARM YOURSELVES!
"THE BERSERKERS. THEY'RE HERE."

RRRRRRMMMMGGGGGGRRRRRMMMMMMGGRRRRRRRR
NO MASKS THIS TIME. TAKE PRIDE IN WHO WE ARE AND WHAT WE STAND FOR.
WHAT THE HELL...

STOP!
IF THEY'RE GOING TO TREAT US LIKE WOLVES, LET'S ACT LIKE WOLVES! BITE BACK!

PARAGON MANSION, SEATTLE.
I ADMIT I HAD LOST FAITH, DEATHSTROKE...
...BUT YOUR WORD IS INDEED YOUR BOND.
CAN THE SAME BE SAID OF YOU?
COMPLETE THE TRANSFER.
WHAT THE HELL IS THIS?
$2,000,000.
THAT'S ME BEING GENEROUS.
YOU AGREED TO ADD FIVE MILLION TO THE PURSE IF I DELIVERED WITHIN A WEEK.
AND I'M AFRAID YOU'RE SEVEN HOURS PAST. A DEAL IS A DEAL.
WE WERE WAYLAID BY A TYPHOON WHEN REFUELING IN MANILA. OTHERWISE--
BE HAPPY YOU GOT ANYTHING. IF LATE, YOU AGREED TO FORFEIT YOUR FEE ENTIRELY.

IF YOUR WORD IS INDEED YOUR BOND, YOU'LL LEAVE WITHOUT ANY TROUBLE.
THERE'S A MAN UNDER THAT MASK. A MAN WHO MUST CARE ABOUT MORE THAN MONEY. HELP ME. PLEASE.
MAKING THE RIGHT CHOICE ISN'T PART OF MY JOB DESCRIPTION.
YOU'RE GOING TO ENSLAVE ME? TREAT ME LIKE SOME EXPENSIVE VINTAGE YOU MIGHT HOARD IN YOUR CELLAR?
SHUT HIM UP, DANA. AND CUT HIM OPEN.
I'M *DYING* FOR A TASTE.

MAYBE IT'S JUST THE ANGER SMOLDERING INSIDE ME...
BUT I THINK I SMELL SMOKE...
AND HEAR THE CREAKY MUSIC OF A BOWSTRING.
SNICK
WHEN I KILL SOMEONE, IT'S USUALLY PERMANENT.
SORRY TO STAIN THAT WHOLE "WORLD'S GREATEST ASSASSIN" THING YOU'VE GOT GOING ON.
WHERE'S DOCTOR MIRACLE?

HE'S A HEALER. NOT SOME IMPERIAL MUMMY'S PERSONAL BLOOD BAG.
FOR ONCE, I'M NOT YOUR ENEMY.
I DELIVERED DOCTOR MIRACLE. PLEASE DO ME THE FAVOR OF UNDELIVERING HIM.
AND WHILE YOU'RE AT IT, JAM THIS BROADHEAD THROUGH THE OLD MAN'S THROAT.
THERE IS A SECTION OF LAKE SUPERIOR WHERE MIGRATING BUTTERFLIES ABRUPTLY CHANGE COURSE.
BECAUSE MILLIONS OF YEARS AGO, A MOUNTAIN ONCE ROSE THERE.
MY FATHER ONCE DID BUSINESS WITH PARAGON, RELYING ON HIM AS A SIGNIFICANT INVESTOR IN QUEEN INDUSTRIES.
AND YET HERE I AM. HEADED DIRECTLY FOR THE OLD MOUNTAIN.
IT'S DIFFICULT TO ESCAPE YOUR INHERITANCE.
BUT NOT IMPOSSIBLE.

MY BLOOD WILL MEND YOU--IT'S TRUE--BUT IT WILL EVENTUALLY CYCLE OUT OF YOUR SYSTEM.
...BECAUSE I PLAN ON LASTING ANOTHER CENTURY.
WELL THEN, I HOPE YOU'RE COMFORTABLE...
I'M READY, DANA. FILL ME WITH MIRACLES.
SHLIKK
SHLIKK
NO! DANA! KILL THEM!

GET THIS THING AWAY FROM ME!
I DON'T KNOW. GEORGE COULD REALLY USE AN OLD BONE TO BURY IN THE BACKYARD.
I WANT TO THANK YOU, BUT I SUSPECT YOU'RE ONLY HERE BECAUSE YOU WANT SOMETHING FROM ME.
IT'S TRUE. I'M SORRY.
I USED TO WISH MORE THAN ANYTHING I WAS GIFTED, SPECIAL, AND THEN--
YOU DISCOVERED THE BURDEN OF POWER?
I WON'T PRETEND TO KNOW MORE THAN A LITTLE ABOUT WHAT YOUR LIFE MUST BE LIKE...
BUT I'M HERE TO ASK FOR HELP. NOT DEMAND IT.

BLAST
SHU-SHUNK
BAD DOG.

ENOUGH!
THIS CAN'T END, BECAUSE THERE'S NO END TO HATE.
THE BEST I CAN OFFER, FOR THOSE WHO WANT IT, IS A CURE.
WHAT DO YOU MEAN, CURE?
ANY INJURY, ANY DISEASE, THIS MAN CAN HEAL.

SHOW ER. SHOW THEM.
DON'T WORRY. I'M HERE TO HELP.
IT'S WORKING...
...THE WOUND IS CLOSING...
...MY VEINS FEEL CHARGED WITH LIGHT.
MOAN
HAVE YOU HEARD? THEY'RE SAYING THERE'S A CURE.
PERSONALLY, I FIND THAT HARD TO SWALLOW.

LET'S RIDE!
I THINK... I MIGHT WANT TO STAY...
YOU'RE NOT GOING TO GO AFTER HIM?
NO.
I'M THINKING A PART OF YOU LIKES THAT HE'S OUT THERE?
THE SICK PART OF YOU THAT NEVER WANTED TO GET WELL.
OR MAYBE IT'S THE PART OF ME THAT BELIEVES CHANGE CAN ONLY COME FROM THE WARRING SIDES OF US.
THE END

VARIANT COVER GALLERY

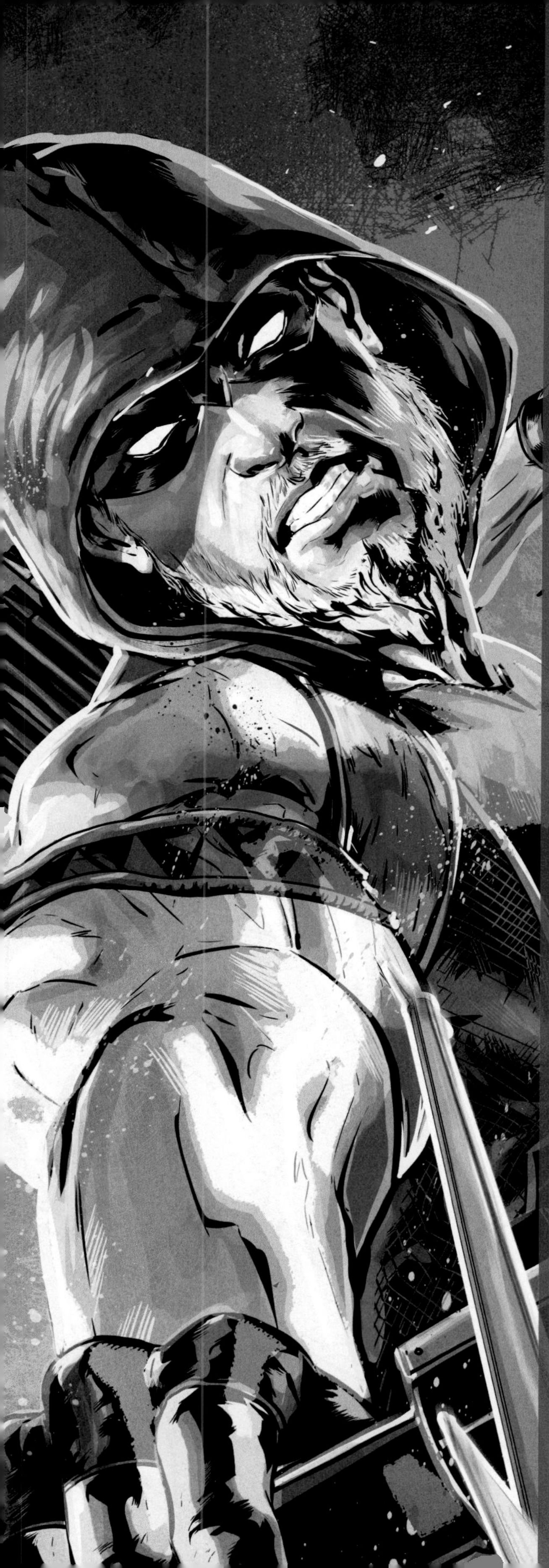

GREEN ARROW 48
ADULT COLORING BOOK VARIANT
BY CULLY HAMNER

GREEN ARROW 49
VARIANT BY NEAL ADAMS,
JIM LEE & ALEX SINCLAIR

GREEN ARROW 50
BATMAN V SUPERMAN VARIANT
BY AARON KUDER
WITH TOMEU MOREY

GREEN ARROW 51
VARIANT BY JOHN ROMITA JR.
AND SCOTT HANNA
WITH DEAN WHITE

GREEN ARROW 52
NEW 52 HOMAGE VARIANT
BY SZYMON KUDRANSKI
(AFTER DAVE WILKINS)

JR JR
S.H.
DW

SZYMON
KUDRANSK

GREEN ARROW™
REBIRTH

The future (and past) of the DC Universe starts with DC UNIVERSE: REBIRTH!

Explore the changing world of Oliver Queen in this in this special bonus of **GREEN ARROW: REBIRTH #1**!

SEATTLE.
"ARE YOU ALONE, MISTER QUEEN?"
"AFRAID SO.
"SHE SAID SHE FOUND ME 'EXHAUSTING.' SHE SAID SHE WAS SICK OF MY 'SANCTIMONIOUS, HOLIER-THAN-THOU *ATTITUDE*.'"
LIBERAL PIG...
"PERHAPS NEXT TIME YOU'LL FIND A BETTER MATCH THAN A *REPUBLICAN SENATOR'S DAUGHTER*."
"HE'S THE KIND OF CONSERVATIVE NUT JOB WHO THINKS GUNS SHOULD HAVE THE RIGHT TO MARRY OTHER GUNS. I DON'T KNOW WHY SHE'S DEFENDING HIM. AND--GET THIS--SHE THINKS MY BEARD IS *GROSS*."
"IF YOU DIDN'T TIP SO WELL, I MIGHT *AGREE* WITH HER. I TRUST YOU ENJOYED YOUR MEAL OTHERWISE?"
A BIT *RICH*, BUT OTHERWISE GOOD.
THANKS, TOMMY.
UNTIL NEXT TIME, MISTER QUEEN. TAKE CARE.
PLEASE?
KILLS FASCISTS

OF COURSE, BUDDY. I HOPE THIS HELPS.
THANK YOU, MISTER BEARD MAN.
WOOOSHH
YOU STAY HERE AND GUARD OUR THINGS.
MOMMY WILL BE RIGHT BACK.
THIS MACHINE KILLS FASCISTS
SLURM SLURM
AAIIIEE
MOMMY?
SLURM
THIS MACHINE KILLS FASCISTS

I CAME HOME TO THE NEWS THAT SEVENTEEN MISSING PERSONS CASES HAVE BEEN FILED WITH THE SEATTLE P.D.
ALL WOMEN AND CHILDREN. ALL POOR, MANY HOMELESS.
A POPULATION THAT OFTEN DOESN'T REPORT CRIMES.
SO SEVENTEEN MIGHT ACTUALLY MEAN THIRTY, EVEN FIFTY.
AAAHHH!
LET ME GO! I WANT MY MOM!
I LIVE TWO LIVES.
THE FIRST, AS OLIVER QUEEN, MIGHT SEEM ENVIABLE, AS I HOVER OVER EVERYONE IN MY PENTHOUSE APARTMENT, MY TOP-FLOOR OFFICE, GOLDEN CUBES OF LIGHT HIGHER THAN FEAR OR DANGER CAN REACH.
BUT WITH EVERY PASSING DAY THAT WORLD FEELS LESS COMFORTABLE, AND THAT MAN--THE PLAYBOY SOCIALITE, THE C.E.O. OF QUEEN INDUSTRIES--FEELS LIKE MORE OF AN OBNOXIOUS STRANGER.
TWAKK
I PREFER THE COMPANY OF THE STREETS. I PREFER THE JOB DESCRIPTION OF SOCIAL JUSTICE WARRIOR.

CALL ME GREEN ARROW.
REBIRTH
STORY BENJAMIN PERCY ART AND COLOR OTTO SCHMIDT LETTERING NATE PIEKOS OF BLAMBOT®
COVER JUAN FERREYRA VARIANT COVER STEVE SKROCE WITH ALEX SINCLAIR GROUP EDITOR BRIAN CUNNINGHAM
ASSOCIATE EDITOR HARVEY RICHARDS EDITOR ANDY KHOURI

DON'T WORRY, BUDDY. I'VE GOT YOU.
TWAK
THAP
WAIT. I KNOW YOU...

...BUT APPARENTLY YOU DON'T RECOGNIZE BLACK CANARY.

I'M SORRY. I THOUGHT--
IT'S ALL RIGHT. WE'VE ONLY MET ONCE BEFORE.
I HARDLY RECOGNIZE YOU MYSELF. HIDDEN UNDER ALL THAT HAIR.
MAYBE YOU CAN HELP US.
HE WANTS HIS MOM, BUT HE NEEDS A NURSE. AND A BATH.

OLIVER QUEEN'S APARTMENT.
WHAT ARE YOU DOING HERE ANYWAY?
I DIDN'T KNOW I NEEDED GREEN ARROW'S PERMISSION TO ENTER SEATTLE.
I MEAN IN THE STREET. ON A RAINY NIGHT. WITH THIS KID.
I HEARD CRYING FROM A SEWER AND FOUND HIM STUCK DOWN THERE. HE SAID HE WAS TRYING TO SAVE HIS MOTHER WHEN HE FELL, SLICED UP HIS ARM ON THE RUSTED GRATE.
HE SAID "THEY" TOOK HER.
THEY? THEY, WHO?
WE WANT TO HELP YOU, BUDDY. CAN YOU HELP US? WHO TOOK YOUR MOM?
THE UNDERGROUND MEN.
MED KIT'S IN THE LINEN CLOSET. AND FOR CLOTHES, CHECK OUT MY SISTER EMI'S ROOM. SOMETHING OF HERS SHOULD FIT.
I'LL BE THERE IN A MINUTE...
THANK YOU, MISTER BEARD MAN!
I JUST WANT TO CLEAN UP.

YOU KNOW THE JUSTICE LEAGUE AND THE GOTHAM CREW, THEY TALK ABOUT YOU. I'M AFRAID YOU'VE GOT A REP AS A SANCTIMONIOUS JERK.
WHAT? I CAN'T HEAR YOU WITH THE WATER RUNNING.
ALWAYS LOUD-MOUTHING YOUR MORAL OUTRAGE, COMPLAINING ABOUT ELITISM, RACISM, CRONYISM, CONSERVATISM, ANY -ISM, ALL THE -ISMS.
YOU CALL YOURSELF A SOCIAL JUSTICE WARRIOR...
BUT LOOK AT THIS APARTMENT. LOOK AT THIS LIFE.
SO? WHAT DO YOU THINK?
TO BE HONEST, I THINK YOU'RE A BIT OF A HYPOCRITE.
HOW CAN YOU FIGHT THE MAN...IF YOU ARE THE MAN?
I MEANT, WHAT DO YOU THINK OF THE GOATEE? I WAS GETTING SICK OF ALL THE BEARD JOKES.
WHAT ARE YOU TALKING ABOUT, "I'M THE MAN"?!
IT MEANS YOU'RE GOING TO HAVE TO DO MORE THAN SHAVE TO IMPRESS ME.
LET'S GET THIS KID HOME. HE SAYS WE CAN FIND HIS FATHER IN THE JUNGLE.
THE WHAT?

THE JUNGLE.
THE JUNGLE IS A HOMELESS ENCAMPMENT THAT REACHES ACROSS SEVERAL HUNDRED ACRES OF GREENBELT. HOW **CHECKED OUT** ARE YOU?
I'VE BEEN ACCUSED OF HAVING AN IMPENETRABLE EGO, BUT MAYBE LET'S QUIT WITH THE INSULTS.
YOU CAN'T JUST SPRINKLE A HUNDRED BUCKS AT EVERY PROBLEM AS IF IT WERE FAIRY DUST AND HOPE FOR THE BEST.
I'M DOING A HELL OF A LOT MORE THAN THAT.
MAYBE. SO FAR SEATTLE APPEARS AS NEGLECTED AS THAT HEROIN-ADDICTED PARTNER YOU USED TO HAVE.
DON'T YOU **DARE** SAY THAT.
YOU PLAY HERO OF THE COMMON MAN IN THE STREETS, THEN YOU GO HOME TO BATHE IN CHAMPAGNE AND SLEEP ON A MATTRESS OF MONEY.
AS IF YOU'VE GOT IT ROUGH, LITTLE MISS **ROCK STAR!**
YOU DON'T KNOW A **THING** ABOUT ME.

YOU DON'T KNOW A THING ABOUT *ME.*
THERE WAS A TIME WHEN I WAS A WORLD-CLASS PRIVILEGED D-BAG, I'LL ADMIT, BUT THEN--
BUT THEN WHAT?
THEN A STORM CAME. THEN MY SHIP SANK. THEN *THE ISLAND* CLAIMED ME. THEN I LEARNED TO SURVIVE.
THEN I LEARNED TO CARE ABOUT SOMEONE OTHER THAN MYSELF.
OKAY, SO MAYBE I DON'T KNOW EVERY-THING.
LIKE HOW MUCH QUEEN INDUSTRIES GIVES TO CHARITY, LIKE HOW MANY PROGRAMS I FUND, LIKE HOW MUCH THE TRICK ARROWS AND THE SURVEILLANCE AND THE LABWORK AND THE SOUPED-UP MOTORCYCLES AND BOATS AND PLANES *COST?* MAKING A DIFFERENCE REQUIRES *MONEY.*
WHY THE HELL AM I EVEN EXPLAINING MYSELF? WHAT DO *YOU* CARE?
I CARE BECAUSE I USED TO *BE* THIS KID.
BOUNCING BETWEEN FOSTER HOMES AND THE STREET.
HOW ABOUT WE TRADE, *HUH?* I'LL TAKE YOUR ISLAND ANY DAY.
DADDY!
BUT WHERE'S YOUR MOTHER?
SHE'S MISSING. AND SHE'S ONE OF MANY. MAYBE YOU CAN HELP US UNDERSTAND WHAT'S HAPPENING.
AAIIIEEEE
IT'S THEM...

"...THE UNDERGROUND MEN."
SLURM
NOOO! HELP!
SLURM
THEY'RE BACK!
SLURM
SLURM
AAAAH!
THESE GUYS LIKE TO STICK TO THE SHADOWS.
SO LET'S STEAL BACK THE NIGHT.
PAF

SNIK
SLURM
THIS IS WHAT IT SOUNDS LIKE...
...WHEN YOUR EARS BLEED.
THERE'S SOMETHING ABOUT HER...SOMETHING THAT MAKES ME FEEL GRATEFULLY DEFENSELESS.
THWAKK

WHAT ARE YOU DOING TO THESE PEOPLE? WHERE ARE YOU TAKING THEM?
I'M NO MUSIC CRITIC, BUT YOU CAN SURE WAIL. THAT WAS KIND OF AMAZING.
NO MATTER HOW MUCH I SCREAM, I DON'T THINK THIS WORM IS GOING TO TALK.
LISTEN, WORM. THERE'S A SPECIAL BLACK CHAMBER IN MY HEART. IT'S FULL OF SHARP OBJECTS, BUT IT'S PRETTY MUCH ABSENT OF MERCY. AND IT'S RESERVED ESPECIALLY FOR THOSE WHO PREY ON THE WEAK.
YOU HAVE FIVE SECONDS, AND THEN I'M GOING TO TAKE YOU THERE FOR A SPECIAL V.I.P. TOUR.
SLURM
TONIGHT...
...THE AUCTION.
WHERE? WHERE'S THIS AUCTION?
THERE...

"...BELOW."
WHY DID YOU COME TO SEATTLE, REALLY?
THOUGHT I MIGHT GO ON A BIT OF A WALKABOUT, HIKE THE PACIFIC CREST TRAIL.
I HEAR THAT'S WHAT PEOPLE ARE DOING THESE DAYS WHEN THEY FEEL LOST AND IN NEED OF REINVENTION.
THAT SOUNDS A LITTLE DRAMATIC, DOESN'T IT? SORRY. I'VE BEEN THROUGH A LOT LATELY.
YOU KNOW WHERE WE ARE? A FAR-REACHING BRANCH OF THE SEATTLE UNDERGROUND, I THINK.
THERE WAS A MASSIVE FIRE BACK IN THE 1800s AND THEY REBUILT THE CITY TWO STORIES ABOVE WHERE IT ONCE STOOD.
SEATTLE WAS REBORN OVER THE ASHES OF ANOTHER TIME.
THE CITY GOT A SECOND CHANCE. I GOT A SECOND CHANCE. SO DO YOU.
HERE'S TO SECOND CHANCES, I GUESS.
ALL RIGHT. NOW FOLLOW THE RICH, ARROGANT LOUDMOUTH...
...WHO MAKES UP FOR HIS INADEQUACIES WITH COOL GADGETS.
PAF
HAPPILY.
I'VE GOT A FEELING THIS TRAIL OF BLOOD...

"...IS GOING TO LEAD TO THE HEART OF THE PROBLEM."
NOT TOO FAR FROM THE DOCKS, BENEATH THE DOWNTOWN, A RUINED MANSION LIES BURIED.
BUILT IN 1887 BY THE HURST FAMILY, TIMBER AND CATTLE BARONS WHO CONTROLLED MORE THAN TEN MILLION ACRES OF THE PACIFIC NORTHWEST.
FIRE IS A GREAT EQUALIZER, AND THE MANSION BURNED ALONG WITH THE REST OF THE CITY.
BUT TODAY THEIR BALLROOM ONCE AGAIN HOSTS THE MONEYED.
BEFORE WE BEGIN, LET ME REMIND YOU THAT THIS FEED IS CAMOUFLAGED BY TWENTY V.P.N. RELAYS...
...THAT WE ONLY ACCEPT LEXCOIN CRYPTOCURRENCY TRANSACTIONS, AND THAT NEXT MONTH'S UNDERGROUND AUCTION WILL BE SOURCED FROM SAN FRANCISCO.
WITHOUT FURTHER ADO, OUR FIRST PROPERTY IS A TWENTY-FIVE-YEAR-OLD FEMALE.
LET'S OPEN THE BIDDING AT TEN THOUSAND. WHETHER YOU FANCY HER FOR WORK, PLEASURE, FOOD, LABORATORY EXPERIMENTATION...
LEXCOIN
15000 | 17500
LEXCOIN
12000 | 15000 | 17500
...REST ASSURED THAT THIS IS A CLEAN EXCHANGE.
NO ONE WILL EVER PURSUE HER OR ANY OF OUR PROPERTIES, BECAUSE THEY ARE NO ONE. SHE IS NO ONE.
THEY'RE COMING!
THEY'RE ALREADY HERE!

THE BIDDING IS CLOSED.
KRNSH
PLAK
UNNH
CHOK

THNK
THUNK
THUNK
YOU THINK THEIR LIVES ARE YOURS TO SELL?
EVERYONE'S LIFE IS FOR SALE. EVEN YOURS.
THESE PEOPLE ARE SO IRRELEVANT THEY MIGHT AS WELL NOT EXIST.
YOU'RE WRONG.
SOMEONE CARES.

SOMEONE CARES.
I MIGHT NOT HAVE ANY SPECIAL POWERS. I MIGHT BE YOUNG, I MIGHT BE A LOUDMOUTH, I MIGHT HAVE A LOT TO LEARN. BUT DON'T UNDERESTIMATE ME.
WHATEVER THIS IS, I'M GOING TO STOP IT. WHOEVER YOU ARE, I'M GOING TO HUNT YOU DOWN.
AND WHEN I DO, I'LL MAKE YOU FEEL DEBASED, DEVALUED, BANKRUPT IN EVERY POSSIBLE WAY.
THERE WILL BE NOTHING LEFT.
YOU'LL KNOW WHAT IT FEELS LIKE TO BE NO ONE.
THUNNK--ZZTT
THAT, I PROMISE.

YOU TOOK ME AND THAT BOY TO YOUR APARTMENT EARLIER. WITHOUT A SECOND THOUGHT.
PROTECTING MY IDENTITY DIDN'T SEEM AS IMPORTANT AS PROTECTING THAT BOY.
I GUESS I WASN'T AFRAID TO REVEAL MYSELF. NOT TO YOU.
AND YET, I DON'T EVEN KNOW YOUR NAME.
DINAH. DINAH LANCE.
OLIVER QUEEN. NICE TO MEET YOU, DINAH...
...FINALLY.
THE BEGINNIN

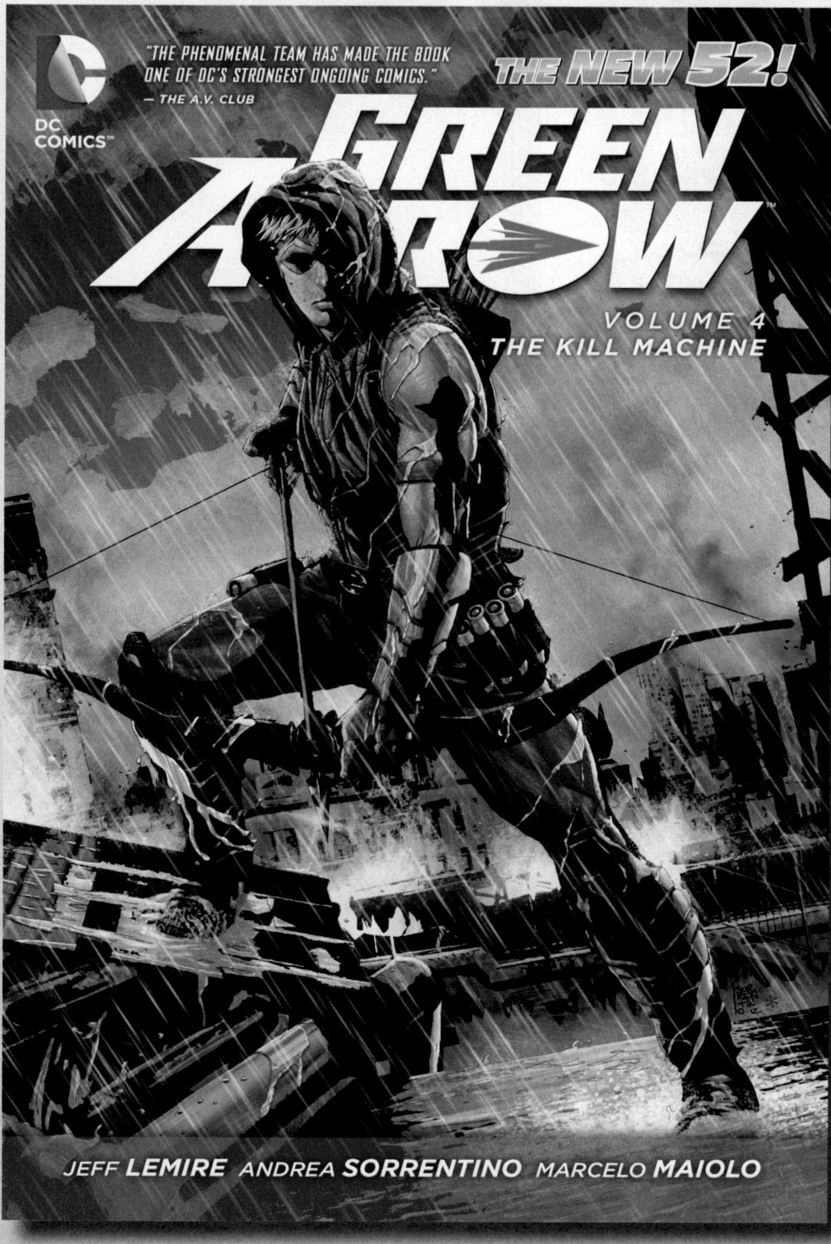
DC COMICS
"THE PHENOMENAL TEAM HAS MADE THE BOOK ONE OF DC'S STRONGEST ONGOING COMICS."
— THE A.V. CLUB
THE NEW 52!
GREEN ARROW
VOLUME 4
THE KILL MACHINE
JEFF LEMIRE ANDREA SORRENTINO MARCELO MAIOLO

THE NEW 52!
GREEN ARROW
VOLUME 1
THE MIDAS TOUCH
DAN JURGENS J.T. KRUL KEITH GIFFEN GEORGE PÉREZ

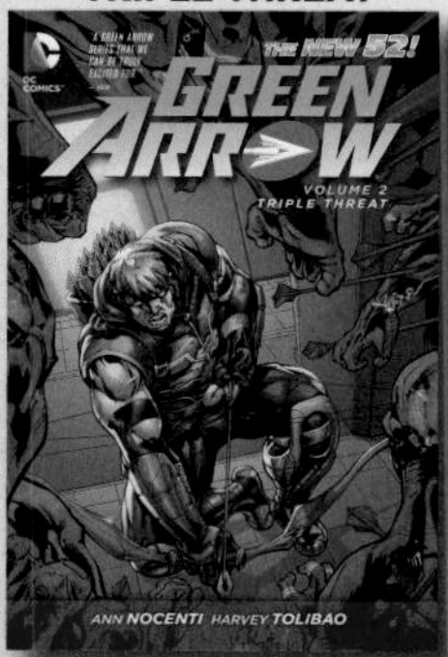
THE NEW 52!
GREEN ARROW
VOLUME 2
TRIPLE THREAT
ANN NOCENTI HARVEY TOLIBAO

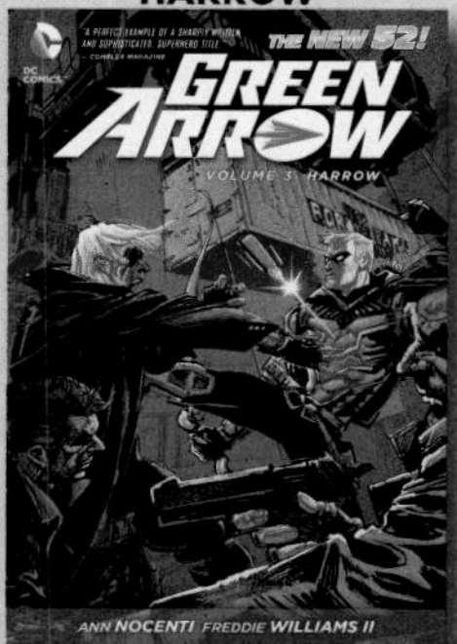
THE NEW 52!
GREEN ARROW
VOLUME 3: HARROW
ANN NOCENTI FREDDIE WILLIAMS II

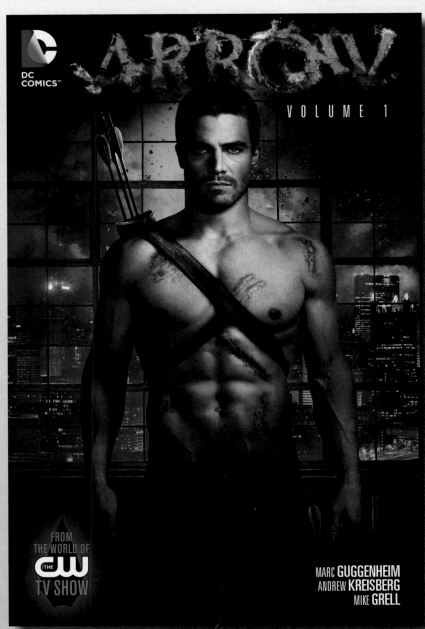

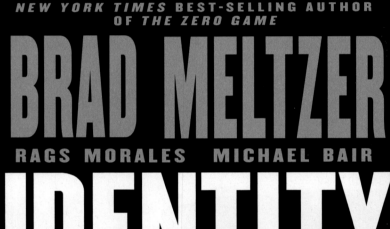